The Critics Rave About Jessica Savitch and ANCHORWOMAN...

"Savitch is classy; she has a punchy style, writes well and when you see the twinkle in her eye as she delivers the news, you'll be reminded of this book."
—Nancy Dickerson,
The Washington Post

"Savitch's book...names names and details of some of the more outrageous episodes en route to the top."
—*Women's Wear Daily*

"...Jessica's most pleasing attribute is a bright and shining intelligence, a grasp of the news, personal relationships and an unmuddled view of herself as a pioneer woman in prime-time network broadcasting."
—New York *Daily News*

"...Success stories such as Savitch's make fascinating reading."
Daily Star

Jessica Savitch
Anchorwoman

BERKLEY BOOKS, NEW YORK

This Berkley book contains the complete
text of the original hardcover edition.

ANCHORWOMAN

A Berkley Book / published by arrangement with
G. P. Putnam's Sons

PRINTING HISTORY
G. P. Putnam's edition / October 1982
Berkley edition / November 1983

ISBN: 0-425-06409-3

A BERKLEY BOOK ® TM 757,375
Berkley Books are published by The Berkley Publishing Group,
200 Madison Avenue, New York, New York 10016.
The name "BERKLEY" and the stylized "B" with design
are trademarks belonging to Berkley Publishing Corporation.
PRINTED IN THE UNITED STATES OF AMERICA

Acknowledgments

Bill Adler: For being the originator

Robert L. Andrews: For his direction

Kenneth H. Bastian, Jr.: For being there . . . and staying

Leila M. Bright: For keeping the author on schedule

David Buda: For his masterful organization

Robyn Capazzi: For on-the-road management

Chewy the Dog: For being woman's best friend

Robert and Katherine Clarke: Keepers of the faith and clip files

Christine Connal: For the new edition tape stories

Mort and Nicki Crim: Great colleagues and wonderful friends

Alan D'Angerio: For his inimitable "style"

Jered Dawaliby and Alise Baer-Dawaliby: Secretarial assistance . . . plus

Joan Durham: For future sight

Ellen Ehrlich: For personal and professional ideals

Pat Garvey and Donna Fitzpatrick: Good Samaritans

Edward Goldberger: For loving memories

Phyllis Grann: For her many editorial insights

Donald Hamburg: For legal assistance "with options"
Barbara King: For professional excellence
Susan LaSalla: Field production mixed with friendship
Richard Leibner: For negotiated victories
Vince and Frankie Leonard: Great colleagues and wonderful friends
Carol Levine: For assistance in projects in the early days
Maury Z. Levy: For knowing the difference between style and substance
Dr. Patricia Payne Mahlstedt: A sister-in-law plus support
Robert Mahlstedt: Support plus a brother-in-law
Mary Manilla: For sharing her experiences and her time
Yvette Margarita Montilla: For Spanish sisterhood
Robert Morse: For inaugurating a very good year
Tracy and Wil Rappaport: For helping with the acknowledgments
Benjamin Savitch: For a genetic edge
Lillian Savitch: My paternal grandmother . . . inspiration, plus David
Stephanie Savitch-Newman: For being a sister . . . friend and critic
Lance and Lori Savitch-Teblum: My brother-in-law and sister . . . with appreciation
Dr. Thomas Sedlacek: For survival
Joan Showalter: For the times she believed for both of us
Sue Simmons: For logic
Tim Skinell: For lessons in British stoicism
Aldemira Spadoni: My maternal grandmother . . . for inspiration . . . and for Florence
Roberta Spring: For assistance above and beyond the call
Sveltie the Cat: Black cat for good luck
Carl and Jean Sylvester: For care and feeding of the author
Ruth Tabron: For clothes made as a labor of love
Faith Ann Thomas: For support from playpens to forever
Tressa Verna: For the first edition tape stories
Diana Walker: For photographic friendship

To My Parents, Florence and David Savitch:
For Life

To D. R. P.: For Love

To Samuel Rappaport: For Truth

To Rita Rappaport: For Friendship

To Brian B. Doyle: For Reality

Prologue

When I was a little girl in the 1950s, it would not have been possible for me to say, "I want to be an anchorwoman when I grow up." No such person existed. The only anchor I had ever seen in my rural Pennsylvania town was John Cameron Swayze on *Camel News Caravan.* I wanted to be a princess—not a flesh and blood Grace Kelly, but a fairy-tale princess, living happily ever after with her Prince Charming.

In the fall of 1979, I was in Nebraska doing a story for *NBC Magazine* on the end of the one-room schoolhouse, and the teacher asked me to talk to a group of third graders. "This is Jessica Savitch. She works for NBC News as an anchor-woman," she said. "Do any of you know the definition of anchorwoman?" Dead silence. Finally from the back row, a towheaded girl tentatively raised her hand. "Uh . . . I think it's when they pay you a lot of money to look pretty and read wo. . on telebishion."

That little girl suddenly made me real.. that anchorwomen are seen as today's princesses. By late 1980, I was receiving an average of twenty letters a day from young people asking how they could get a job like mine. Their reasons, all too often, were fame, fortune, and a glamorous life. In short, they wanted to get paid a lot of money for looking pretty and reading words on television.

Barely a decade ago, the term "anchorwoman" was virtually nonexistent. In 1970 a scattering of women at various local stations across America were named solo or co-anchors of midday, early morning or weekend newscasts. (Prime time was still an all-male domain.) Reportedly, I was the first in the South. A regional oddity. The subject of a variety of interviews.

The first interviewer asked me what I was going to call myself. Having struggled along with "Jessica Savitch" for some twenty years, I told him I planned to use my own name.

"No," he explained. "I mean what are you going to call your job title . . . A woman anchoring the news can't exactly be a female anchorman."

"How about anchorwoman?" I ventured.

"It's sexist," he rejoined.

I told him if he could figure out a title for a female anchor, I'd go along.

The headline in the newspaper the following day read JESSICA SAVITCH: SOUTH'S FIRST ANCHORONE.

I sent the newspaper on to my mother and sisters, who were not especially impressed. What, they asked me, is an ancho-RONE anyway?

Thereafter I decided to forego the title anchor-ONE in favor of anchorwoman. Not only does it make a readable headline, it makes the point that one is not biologically predestined to renounce one's femininity in order to be promoted to anchor.

While I recognize that anyone who writes an autobiographical work at the age of thirty-four is, at best, presumptuous, it occurred to me that it was time to set the record straight. From the beginning of my career, I kept journals and scrapbooks chronicling what was to be a hilarious, exhilarating, and often infuriating journey across uncharted territory. My intention was to wait until I had achieved a comfortable retirement sometime in the distant future and then write a book for those young women who would and ought to follow. A number of factors accelerated my time schedule, but one of the most important was my discovery that, because I was an unwitting pioneer in my field, I had become a role model.

In fact, this book really began the day I set out

on Old Turnpike Road in Pleasantville, New Jersey, to begin work as a high school reporter on a weekly radio program called *Teensville*. I was the first female in the history of the station to hold the job, and I was to discover that there were few women working *anywhere* in the broadcast industry. In the nineteen years since I pedaled my blue three-speed bike to WOND, the changes in the industry have been nothing short of phenomenal. Changes in legislation and technology; changes in the importance of the newscast and, concomitantly, the newscaster; changes, at long last, in attitudes toward women and minorities.

In early 1981 I discussed this book with my soon-to-be husband, Donald Rollie Payne, a forty-four-year-old Texas-born doctor with dark, sparkling eyes and a pirate's smile—an intelligent, compassionate person who was my best friend. Doing the book would mean giving up just a little bit more of the privacy we both had tried so hard to preserve. We spent a good many evenings arguing the pros and cons. In the end we decided there was a need for a realistic overview of the personal and professional demands of broadcasting. With Donald's support I began the book, only to be interrupted by a tragedy neither of us could have foreseen. Shortly after our marriage, a recurrence of a liver ailment caused my husband's health to deteriorate and after a lengthy hospital stay . . . he ended his life in early August of 1981.

For a time I was devastated. I put the book aside and barely was able to handle my appearances for NBC. But work proved to be the panacea, and with the aid and support of my family, my friends, and my colleagues, eventually I picked up the manuscript again.

When such occurrences in one's personal life overshadow professional events, then, as Marshall McLuhan would say, the messenger is the message. One must "say something"—confront the event, acknowledge it—and go on. I have tried to follow this advice in my life and in this book. But the story I want to tell is not about personal tragedy. For the thousands of viewers who sent me letters of sympathy and encouragement and the hundreds of young women fascinated by the burgeoning field of communications, I want to describe the adventures of a television career—of an anchorwoman, a new term for a new time.

Chapter
1

In 1954 my father, a clothing store merchant, bought us our first television. He was an ardent fan of Edward R. Murrow, and I have a hazy memory of hearing him talk about Murrow's documentary on migrants, *Harvest of Shame*, a classic I was to study years later in college. Although my father was a folksy man, he was never one to engage in kid talk. Over our all-American dinners of meat-loaf and canned peas and fruit cocktail, he talked to me about current events—sober, grown-up discussions of Eisenhower, Hoffa, desegregation in Selma. I conscientiously studied my *Weekly Readers* so I would have something to contribute to our nightly ritual, and straightaway I discovered television news. It was to win his approval that I began to follow news events, but in time I became mesmerized by the stories themselves.

The year I turned twelve, my father became gravely ill with a kidney disease, and his death, at the age of thirty-three, shattered my life.

My mother was forced to sell the house and move us from the Kennett Square area to Margate, New Jersey, to be near her parents, who lived on the seashore. I felt like Dorothy in *The Wizard of Oz*, swept away by the tornado to a strange land. Everything familiar to me was gone: my father, my home, my school, my community, my friends, and even, in a way, my mother, who resumed the nursing career she had abandoned when she married. (She had been a nurse in the Navy, where she met my father, a pharmacist's mate.) Supporting three young girls became an increasing struggle; it was a shock to find out that the first time I wanted a party dress, we could not afford it—nor could we afford a lot of party dresses thereafter.

I entered Atlantic City High School, a monstrous, noisy inner-city school with an ethnic and socio-economic mix that confounded me. I was used to the tidy homogeneity of my provincial school in Pennsylvania. Here in Atlantic City my classmates were sons and daughters of wealthy merchants; blacks from the ghetto; street-wise urbanites who must surely have recognized that I, with my hopeless knee socks that didn't always match my sweaters, was as out of place as I felt.

By happenstance, I sat next to a boy in one of my sophomore classes named Steve Berger, who worked for a weekend AM radio show in Pleasantville called *Teensville*. From the moment he told me about it, I was captivated by the idea. On a Saturday morning I drove with Steve across the bridge to the WOND station, a faded saltbox on stilts known affectionately as "The Jukebox in the Swamp." Steve introduced me to the program director, Mike Elliott, who asked if I would like to record an introduction to the afternoon show. When I got home my mother and I listened to the program at the kitchen table; as soon as I heard my voice on the airwaves, my destiny was fixed. I sent an application to Mike Elliott, and was chosen for a weekend position—called reporter by courtesy only. The show was little more than back-to-back music, so the only skill required was to spin records and read the news summary every hour. A couple of minutes before the hour, I raced down the hall, ripped the copy off the wire machine, raced back before the record ended and read the news on the air (known in the trade as Rip 'n' Read). Since there was no time to study the copy beforehand, I simply plunged in and read it cold. I learned early on that being a news reader—as opposed to reporter—is a risky proposition at best. My most common gaffe was stumbling over unfamiliar words; my worst was reading the "continued on next graph" that appeared at the bottom of each page. "In response to questions on the city's sewage problem, the mayor continued on next graph . . ." (pause, turn the page) ". . . said he was working with the city council . . ."

A fellow reporter once told me that while reading the news, he came upon the story of an African leader who had been killed whose name was a long, tongue-twisting series of consonants. Realizing he couldn't pronounce it, my friend sputtered and said, "His name is being withheld pending notification of the next of kin."

I was not only the announcer, newscaster and record-spinner, I was the engineer, transmitter-reader and remote-broadcast technician. The latter category gave me some trouble. One hot summer day, instead of throwing the correct combination of levers to present the listeners with the dulcet tones of the Ray Freeman Pool Party at Atlantic City's Deauville Hotel, I somehow managed to assault them with the pre-taped air raid emergency alert. Fortunately, before Southern New Jersey had its own version of Orson Welles's "War of the Worlds," Program Director Mike Elliott burst in and untangled the technical snafu.

Events like that one aside, I loved everything about the radio station, even its oddly comforting smell of musty records and ink drying on the wire machines and oxidized tapes and marsh gas.

WOND became my center, taking the place of all I had lost. At last I felt as though I belonged. (Radio stations everywhere seem to attract misfits, mildly offbeat types who haven't quite made it into the social mainstream. I once had a radio engineer who maintained a daily practice of bringing in two cups of coffee, opening the first, spilling it on his program log notes and then drinking the second. Asked why, he always said, "Since I would have managed to knock my coffee on my log notes at some point during the day, I try to get it over with first thing and avoid being upset about it later." It is no wonder these wonderful characters make for a hit television series like *WKRP in Cincinnati*.)

In the beginning, my mother humored me when I told her I wanted to be a reporter. "Fine," she would say, smiling distractedly. Before long she grew concerned about the time I was spending at the station ("Why can't you go out to dances like other girls?") and apprehensive over the irritating repetitiveness with which I kept reminding her of my plan.

My dreams of being a reporter took on an aura of reality in the summer of 1964. Atlantic City was the site of the Democratic National Convention, and because WOND was an ABC affiliate, I managed to get a perimeter press pass to Bader Field, the airstrip where Lyndon Johnson would be landing. That press card was like a ticket to paradise. Knees shaking, I drove out to await the plane's descent, wearing high heels and overdone makeup—my useless attempt to look sophisticated.

The image that is limned in my mind is that of Nancy Dickerson standing in the muggy heat of the press pen, looking cool and serene in her pink linen suit, pearls, and Jackie Kennedy bouffant. While the other reporters pushed and shoved and jockeyed for position, she simply raised her hand. LBJ noticed her immediately. "Hi, Nancy," he drawled, and answered her question first. I no longer remember what she asked, only that, in her calm, self-possessed way, she commanded the attention of the president, who called her by name.

Had Nancy Dickerson been on television more often, she might easily have become my idol. But the broadcasting world was almost exclusively male territory. "Women have to work twice as hard and run twice as fast," Nancy Dickerson was once quoted as saying, "to prove they're half as good as any man on the job." The only other women I had seen on air nationally in jobs of any consequence were Barbara Walters and Pauline Frederick. Barbara Walters was not then a co-host on *Today,* and would not be, in fact, for years to come. She was sort of a "Ta-da lady" for the show's male host, as the lady in pink tights who adds a trumpeting flourish when the magician does his tricks. The interviews that eventually made a name for her were those she *fought* to do. Pauline Frederick was the correspondent for the United Nations, an assignment she got because no one else really wanted it. Until Khrushchev's shoe-banging antics in the U.N. and the heating up of the Cold War, the beat was considered a sinecure.

Women were seldom given quality assignments or adequate air time. Most were consigned to the ghetto of so-called women's programs: chatty, lightweight midday features on fashion, food, and other fluff. They were offered scant opportunity to prove their journalistic worth or to set any kind of durable precedent for a fresh, emerging young audience. You might be a champion swimmer, but if you can never get out of the bathtub, what difference does it make? I had no role models because there *were* none.

Nonetheless, I remained determined to make broadcasting my career. By the time the middle of my senior year rolled around, my mother had become outright alarmed. She would have thought me no less delirious had I wanted to be a trapeze artist. There was no frame of reference in my family for a journalistic career of any sort. I was never drawn to print reporting, although it might have been more acceptable to my mother because it was at least a known quantity. The broadcasting field was so new that when she told our next-door neighbor that I planned to study radio and television after graduation, the neighbor exclaimed,

"Terrific! Do you think she'll be able to fix that old set of ours in the den?"

My mother was insistent that I go to Montclair State Teacher's College in New Jersey, because a teaching degree was something I could "fall back on," as her nursing degree had been. She would not give me money, she declared, to pursue this whimsy of mine. I became doleful, then petulant, then sullen, not speaking to her for weeks on end. I called my grandparents in Kennett Square, Pennsylvania, sure they would take my side. They understood why I didn't want to be a teacher, but they had their own notions about my future: I should go to an Ivy League school where the best husband material was being educated and where I could get an MRS along with a BA or BS. Finally, worn down by my incorrigibility, my mother agreed to let me pursue what was then an obscure major called communications—but I would have to find the means to pay for most of my schooling on my own.

I applied to Emerson in Boston, to Syracuse University, and to Ithaca College in upstate New York, all of which had reasonably good communications departments. In the mid-sixties, few schools had communications departments at all. New Jersey had none, which posed a serious problem. I was entitled to a state veteran's scholarship along with a national veteran's scholarship because my father had served in the Navy. However, the state scholarship could only be used in the student's home state. I so desperately needed it that I applied anyway, explaining in a letter to the reviewing board that, considering the unusual circumstances, mine was a special case. To my astonishment, they agreed: I would be allowed to use the scholarship at the school of my choice. Ultimately I chose Ithaca because I was offered a $500 merit scholarship and because it was less expensive than either Emerson or Syracuse. My three scholarships amounted to slightly more than one-quarter of the amount I needed to get through the year.

The summer after high school I worked at two jobs to save money—afternoons and weekends at WOND, and mornings as a switchboard operator at the Coronet Motel near the Boardwalk. The former brought me experience and a measure of local acclaim; the latter brought me a pink slip for my tendency to Centrex nearly 50 percent of incoming calls into oblivion.

Chapter
2

I arrived at Ithaca College, welcomed by my housemother, the suitably decorous Mrs. Hogan. When I was interviewed some months earlier, I was shown modern housing on South Hill, within sight of Cayuga Lake and Cornell. My dorm, however, was a tottering, two-story house located on a downtown street near the communications department, which had not yet been relocated onto the main campus. Ithaca College was under renovation and construction all four years I was there. In brochures of that period, the same lonely shrub appears in photos taken outside a classroom, the gym, and the student union. We dubbed this lone bit of greenery "the everywhere bush." I can only guess that the administration kept digging it up and moving it about. The grounds were mud and exposed rock, not at all the sleek, landscaped green it is today.

I shared a room with three other women; together we were the entire female enrollment in radio-television (one of them, Judith Girard, today is program director for WTAE-TV in Pittsburgh). The college AM-FM station was run by upperclassmen, with rudimentary courses offered in use of the equipment—but I already had my third-class broadcast restricted radio-telephone operator's license, a prerequisite for my work at WOND.

As soon as I settled in, I went over to the station to find out what I had to do in order to start working as an announcer. I was stopped cold. The facilities, they sniffed, were needed to train the men. There were no openings for women on air. I could however, write copy or do public service announcements if I liked. I was flabbergasted. How could they enforce a policy so monumentally unfair? I protested to one of the three professors who served as station advisers. Part of my tuition, I reminded him, was paying for this facility. "Let me save you some time and money," he said with a grin. "There's no place for broads in broadcasting."

Now I was enraged. I complained to the administration: Not only was this unfair treatment, it was out-and-out discrimination. On the instant I got a reputation as a troublemaker—but I also got the job. I was offered the Friday night shift, which they knew would be impossible since it lasted until midnight; curfew for freshmen was 11:00. When I requested Saturdays, it took them aback, probably because they assumed I would prefer dating on weekends.

The Monday after my first Saturday night on the job, I was eating breakfast in the cafeteria when I noticed a table of upperclassmen looking at me and laughing. A moment later one of them got up, walked over, and recited an obviously rehearsed speech: "I am afraid I must present you with this citation. You are hereby barred from broadcasting at our radio facilities for the remainder of the year due to a violation of our policy. You did not fulfill your obligation to record a final meter reading and shut the transmitter down." I had been sidelined on a technicality. They had conveniently omitted to tell me that shutting the transmitter down was part of my job. Sick and humiliated, I stumbled back to my room, fell on the bed, and sobbed. Years later, the same upperclassman who engineered this railroad job called looking for a job.

"Listen, Jessica," he told me, "I've really changed along with the times. I mean, I've even married a woman cameraman."

That November, I made my first television appearance in a student production of what I would later learn was the quintessence of newscasting—election night coverage. Tony Busch, a clean-cut, bespectacled fraternity boy, was directing this rather rustic tally of Tompkins County votes. I went to the rehearsals defiantly dishabille, having adopted an I'll-manage-without-them attitude. "Who's that skinny girl who looks like she just woke up?" I overheard Tony whisper to someone. He was intrigued enough, apparently, to come over and introduce himself. We chatted for a while, and he told me if I would fix myself up, he would give me an on-air part.

When finally I went before the cameras on election night, I swung around to write the returns on the blackboard behind me, only to have the board fall smack on top of me. (That was my introduction to the art of maintaining poise while making an on-air recovery.) Tony thought it was hilarious. Even I could see its humor, but what surprised me more than my talent for burlesque was my affinity for the camera. At the end of the program, I felt the breathless elation of new opportunities. I dated Tony for the next two years (he returned to his hometown of Rochester, 60 miles from Ithaca, after his graduation) and it is to him I owe my break into modeling—the work that provided the money I needed to pay for my education.

Tony introduced me to Bill Schwing, who produced local commercials in the Rochester area at his mobile videotape facility, and to Mike Verno and Ann Rogers, who headed ad agencies. I began by doing voice-overs (off-camera audio parts in which you are heard but not seen) and then did on- and off-camera commercials for Marine Midland Bank, Taylor Wine, Star Markets, and a host of local businesses, as well as industrial filmstrips for Kodak, Bausch & Lomb, and R. T. French. Television modeling and voice-overs were a bonanza for me: Some commercials paid as much as $700 plus residuals.

My most lucrative job was a stint as the regional Dodge Girl, a poor man's version of *The Perils of Pauline* stunts made famous by the national Dodge Girl, Pamela Austin. Ours were occasionally ludicrous, and often harrowing. One in particular called for me and the local Dodge dealer to jump a gleaming new car on horseback. I, in my white boots and red cowgirl outfit, barely cleared the Dodge. Dan, the dealer, did *not*. His horse grazed the roof with its hooves, shied, and careened into *my* horse. Both of us took off, bounding madly across the fields of suburban Rochester. Within a few minutes my horse stopped short, hurtling me onto a mound of soft dirt.

Jack Palvino, program director for WBBF in

Rochester, did the voice-over on one of my commercials, and when he found out I had worked for a radio station in high school, he suggested I audition for him. Female disc jockeys were a rarity, and Jack must surely have sensed I could be a salable commodity. He gave me a weekend job at WBBF.

Chapter
3

Known as the Honeybee because of the double
"Bs" in the WBBF call letters, I was sent out to do
live remotes at store openings, special sales, walk-
athons, giveaways, any place or event looking for
promotion. I was a big attention getter, not least
because I operated from a bizarre, glass-enclosed
van called the Beemobile. On top of the
Beemobile was the beehive, a brownish-yellow
heap of plastic that more closely resembled a huge
cow chip. In the dead of summer, trapped beneath this dark, earthy mound, the Beemobile became a blazing inferno. If the air conditioner was
turned on, there was not enough power to spin
records; if the doors were opened to let in cross-
ventilation, curious onlookers were likely to

wander in. "This is the Honeybee," I once announced over the airwaves, "And now for this week's number one hit . . ." as the needle made a sort of *bloop* sound sliding across the grooves. "Sorry! I guess the number one song is tired out from all the air play it's been getting this week! So let's try . . . number five!" The records were actually melting from the heat.

I was frequently the target of young pranksters, such as the boy who stripped down to his bathing trunks and, held aloft by his friends, swam back and forth across my field of vision trying to get me to laugh. Sometimes the merrymaking turned menacing. One Saturday I covered the opening of a store in an outlying section of town. I was scheduled to stay until 6:00. Promptly at 5:00, the store closed, shutting off its main lights. Left alone in the darkening parking lot, I watched as the last of the employees left for the day. Then, coming towards the Beemobile, I spotted a group of seven or eight swaggering hooligans. They surrounded me, dancing to the music, yelling catcalls, writing messages on the glass: "Hi, honey, watcha doin' after the show? How 'bout a little action?" I ignored them, hoping they would get bored and go away. All of a sudden the Beemobile listed violently to the right. One of them had jumped on the front fender. Another pounced on the back to get some rhythms going. Back and forth they seesawed, beginning to frighten me. I couldn't reach the engineer back at the station because the transmitter on my call-back wasn't working, I could only receive messages. I would have to surreptitiously deliver an SOS on the air; but how does one fit Mayday into a music broadcast? "The store is now closed for the night," I said into the mike. "Only a few people are left, actually a bunch of rowdies gathered around me here. That rock 'n' roll you hear is not just the music—it's those rowdies, rocking the Beemobile." The engineer was obviously not listening to my words. He was just waiting for my voice to stop so he could play the commercial. Finally, we were rocking so hard the record jumped and that woke him up. "Are you telling me people are attacking the Beemobile?" he said over the call-back. I answered on the airwaves, "Right! And now for another top hit of the week!" Before the record was finished, a couple of dour policemen arrived and ran the sheepish boys away.

———— • ————

My Beemobile weekends had a certain corny appeal: I signed and gave away albums, handed out fuzzy black-and-yellow bees, had my picture taken with store owners and passersby (me beaming an extravagant, gritted-teeth, Gloria Vanderbilt smile). In time, I picked up some basic interview techniques talking to customers at places like Happy Harry's House of Pancakes or Joe's Pontiac.

"Hi. Have you been to Joe's before?"

"Yes."

"You like the cars?"

"Sure."

"Have you ever bought a car here?"

"Uh-huh."

"How many?"

"Three."

"And all three have been good cars?"

"Right."

"That's nice. OK, thank you."

Those were my first interviews, but they eventually taught me how to ask questions that require more than answers of one syllable. I also learned to keep holding the microphone out a few seconds after the person first finished talking, because that's when he's liable to really open up.

I also learned about sports broadcasting during my Beemobile days. Sports was broadcast a quarter after and quarter of the hour. I studied sports magazines and talked to sports experts in order to brush up on my techniques. I wrote down terms like trounced, squashed, edged out, battered, in order to flavor my reports. I did just fine until my first baseball game went beyond nine innings. Two hundred sixteen irate listeners informed me that the correct phrase is "extra innings," not "overtime."

I really learned the power of the media one sultry Saturday when I played a song by a group called The Popsicles and offhandedly said on air, "Boy, I could sure use a Popsicle myself." The next thing I knew listeners were converging on the Beemobile with single Popsicles, six packs of Popsicles, whole shopping bags of Popsicles. Watching my cache of goods melt into gooey rivers, I finally had to announce, "Enough!"

During Christmas season of 1981, filling in for Tom Brokaw, I co-anchored the *Today Show* with Jane Pauley. We did a story on unusual Christmas gifts, giving special attention to the delightful gadgetry of a Swiss army knife. Both of us, according to *Today* Executive Producer Steve Friedman, received enough knives to supply the Swiss army.

Chapter
4

Between commercials and weekends as the Honeybee, I was spending more time in Rochester than in class. I didn't mind too much since the Ithaca College communications department back then seemed to have arrested its growth somewhere in the 1950s. There had not been much call for my skill at crumpling paper to make it sound like a crackling fire, or thumping my fingertips in imitation of a galloping horse. Both of these techniques I learned in a radio drama course (there has likewise not been much call for my knowledge of radio drama).

The only textbook at that time on television was already outdated, even though it was only four or five years old. It is impossible to produce a book on TV production fast enough to keep up with the rapid-fire technological advances that continue to alter the industry year by year. Today Ithaca has a fine, modern communications facility with updated material and attitudes. It is my honor and pleasure to serve on its board of trustees and as a part-time member of the Communications Department faculty.

Some weeks I commuted almost every day to Rochester, a routine that was becoming monotonous. On Saturday evenings, I often stayed with Bill and Louise Schwing, trading baby-sitting services with Tracy and little Buzzy for room and board. Sundays I got into the habit of stopping over in Geneva, a town at the halfway juncture, to spend the night with Dr. Martin Rand, a psychology professor, and his wife Jo.

The Rands were surrogate parents for an extended family of students, an eclectic mix that might include, at any given point, undergraduates, doctoral candidates, and those stranded during holidays. Martin was a tall, solidly built, convivial man and Jo an earthy woman with large, expressive brown eyes and natural red hair. I, like everyone else, was drawn to their warm-hearted hospitality. They filled in for the family that I missed.

Upon my graduation from Ithaca in 1968, Martin and Jo hosted a party for me. It was a day memorable mostly for its misadventures. A deluge of rain that morning forced the graduation ceremony—for years an outdoor event—inside the gymnasium. There was standing room only, and because there were so many of us, the administration decided simply to read our names off rather than have us receive our diplomas one by one on stage. The audience was asked to refrain from clapping until the list was finished, and everyone complied—until they heard the name Saunders, Steven—magna cum laude, star athlete, class officer and all-around wonderful guy. A spontaneous roar of applause deafened the gym, thereby drowning out the next name, Savitch, Jessica B. It wasn't until I received an honorary doctorate ten years later that my mother actually saw me presented with a sheepskin.

The reception that evening at the Rands' was a cozy affair attended by my mother and sister Stephanie, my grandparents from Kennett Square, my high school girl friend Rusty Nichol, and my date, Jeff Wheat. I was giddy with relief and after a few glasses of champagne the room started to sway. My family and friends undulated around me in a dizzying blur. I sank into a chair. The next thing I knew it was dawn. It was time to recover from my first hangover and look for work. Of the two, the hangover recovery was by far the less painful.

———— • ————

That summer I returned to Rochester to work at WBBF. In my spare time, I sent resumés to at least two dozen radio and television stations in New York, both local and network, sure that with my diploma and my documented experience I would have no problem finding a job. About this time the courts ordered all stations to show what they were doing to implement the progress of minorities, and everybody was looking for qualified blacks to hire. On one interview I was told, "If you were black, I could kill two birds with one stone. I could include you in the woman category, also." On another, that my credentials were not strong enough for the desk assistant's job. The next day a black man was hired who had never been to college. All this was a putdown to me and a putdown to blacks because neither of us should have been judged on the quota system of skin color or sex.

I was to discover over the next few months that a wide range of myths about women persisted in the industry. Women didn't want to watch other women on television because they were jealous of their husbands' diverted attention. Women's voices were not authoritative: meaning that if a male broadcaster said, "Good evening. Two 747s collided in midair today," the viewers would listen and think how tragic. If a female newscaster were to say "Good evening. Two 747s collided in midair today," the viewers would say, "I don't believe it. Not from a *woman*." I remember Archie Bunker telling Edith that he didn't like female newscasters because they had the kind of voices that were made to say things like, "Would you care for another piece of lemon meringue pie?" When he learned about political scandal, war, or fire, he wanted to hear it from a man. After all, he said, men *made* the disasters; they should be the ones to talk about them. There was a lot of Archie Bunker in this business when I started—and alas, still is.

The myths had two things in common: They were fostered by male executives, and there was not a shred of evidence to back them up. How could it be determined that women did not want to watch other women deliver news when they had yet to see any? And if indeed their voices were not perceived as authoritative, could it be because no authority had ever been vested in women?

I was turned down for a variety of other specious reasons, among them that women couldn't work late, that the crew wouldn't want to go out in the field with a woman, that I would cause dissension in the newsroom because I was too pretty. I had made up my mind that I would never be a cookie correspondent; I was not going to teach an audience how to make meatloaf or how to paste on false eyelashes. But such jobs were, by and large, all that women were offered.

I sent letters to other stations outside New York, and I finally got a casual reply from WBZ in Boston. If anyone even *intimated* he would see me, ("If ever in your travels you find yourself in the area, give us a call"), I would be there the next day. Jeff Greenhawt, a high-school classmate who had also worked at WOND, had gone to Emerson College and was living on Beacon Hill. Now owner of a small radio station in York, Pa., Jeff at that time was still struggling to find his own career path. Nonetheless, he made time to meet me at the Greyhound bus station and drive me to the interview. Squire Rushnell, now head of ABC programming, interviewed me: "This is a tough business to break into," he began (that was always the first statement I heard). He didn't hire me, but he spent about an hour with me that afternoon, showing me around the news set. Afterwards I took a cab over to Jeff's.

"How'd it go?" he asked.

"Really well."

"Did you get the job?"

"No."

"Then how could it have gone well?"

"I think he took me seriously."

The time he gave me was my first hint of encouragement. But I still didn't have a job.

Chapter
5

That September I moved to New York City, into a down-and-out women's hotel on East 36th Street. Men were not allowed to visit women in their rooms, so there were always gentleman callers, which is how the telephone operators and desk clerks referred to them, milling about the lobby. For $65 a week I got a room with a narrow, cotlike bed, a dresser, a small wooden desk and chair, a sink, mirror, and tin locker. Also included were breakfast and dinner, although their amorphous gray anonymity made them almost identical. On each floor, dormitory style, were two phones and a large communal bathroom where aspiring models and actresses congregated to experiment with new shades of eyeshadow. Day after day they lugged around their leather portfolios, the most expensive items they owned. Nobody at the hotel had money—if we had, we would have been someplace else. A few had stayed on past the point of transience—sad, middle-aged women who had abandoned their dreams long ago. Next door to me was a cheerful hippie from Kansas named Lisa, who played her guitar long into the night. Soon after I moved in she gave up her quest to become a rock singer and returned to Kansas to work as a computer programmer. "It just seems like the thing to do," she admitted.

I was still doing the Star Market commercials and an occasional industrial filmstrip to support myself, while closely monitoring my modest savings account. I registered with casting directors at all the major ad agencies for commercials, calling them regularly to find out if there were any auditions on. They sent me on a round of cattle calls, joining scores of other hopefuls. Cattle calls are aptly named: You feel as though you're about to have USDA stamped on your thigh as you're stampeded into a corral.

I am not quite 5'5", although in my heart I will always be 5'8", so I couldn't do runway work, nor did I want to take assignments that would send me out of the country. Once, an Easter break did coincide with an assignment in Puerto Rico to do a test market pilot for a diet chocolate soda commercial. They had recruited a group of models—standard blondes-tossing-beach-balls—and sent us down two days ahead of schedule to get our tans going. In the hotel lobby I spotted something called a tan-through bikini, a flimsy flesh-colored suit that allowed the sun's rays to penetrate the garment. It lived up to its advertising, including the part I didn't read. I swam two lengths of the pool and emerged all aglisten to a crowd of open-mouthed stares. My $9 bikini, a paperlike invention, had disintegrated in the water. What do you hide when everything is hanging out? Your face. I dove for my towel and never showed up at the pool again.

I was always a bit uncomfortable modeling, and did it strictly for the money. It seemed a hard way to earn a living; in what other industry does your career start so young and end so young? It made such an impression on me that I later did a special with Tom Snyder on *Prime Time Sunday* called "The Great Modeling War" about new agencies invading the stronghold turf of Ford and Wilhelmina.

I also got a few voice-overs for sales demos and modeled briefly for Clairol. But every time I took these jobs I grew increasingly afraid that my mother might have been right, after all.

By a serendipitous turn of events, I met the woman who was to become my mentor, Joan Showalter, personnel director for CBS. She responded warmly to my letter, and agreed to see me. A Virginia expatriate, Joan had the gracious characteristics of the southern belle, a momentary distraction from her keen intelligence and clear business ability. She showed a sincere interest in my ambitions and was sympathetic to what I was going through. I spilled out all my frustrations in her office. Why was it such a tall order to want to be a broadcast reporter? I was willing to work hard, I was willing to move, I was willing to work for a small salary. All I wanted was a chance to prove I could do the job.

Although discrimination was worse in news than in any other area of television, Joan assured me that it was only a matter of time before things changed. She honestly believed I could go as far as I wanted if I just stuck with it. But there were no reporting jobs for me at CBS. Even openings for production assistants were few and far between, since New York was not then the production center of the industry. Other than soap operas, news, and an occasional talk or variety show, most programs originated in California.

In the end, Joan herself hired me at $92.50 a week to "float" from department to department as an administrative assistant even though I could neither type nor take shorthand. When inevitably the person for whom I was working discovered my nonexistent secretarial skills, Joan plugged me in someplace else. My nondescript "A" position, one of the catch-all jobs women usually got—assistant, associate, alternate—included being sent to the Chinese laundry to pick up a local anchorman's shirts and ordering three-drawer file cabinets for Fred Silverman. Silverman was considered a *wunderkind* even then; in fact, his stint at CBS marked the beginning of his meteoric rise into the executive ranks of television. When he took over as president of NBC, he was still the same youthful, frenetic, heavy-smoking man I remembered—and he is one of the few who remembered *me* from my first job. The CBS offices were in two locations, on 52nd Street where I worked, and in a converted barn on 55th between 9th and 10th Avenues. A shuttle bus went back and forth, and I was occasionally sent to pick up or deliver packages. One day I stopped in the commissary for coffee and met a soap opera star. Later that week I had drinks with him at Top of the Sixes on 5th Avenue—a pleasant enough evening, but my one and only date with him. I was back in the familiar pattern of having to refuse most invitations, since I had enrolled in graduate school at New York University on a tuition reimbursement program.

For approved courses, CBS refunded tuition at the end of each semester if you maintained a B average, so three nights a week I studied political science and took electives like History of the Cinema, a great way to see free movies while also learning the tricks of the camera. Late afternoons I walked to school, going down 5th Avenue to window shop. After passing 34th Street, I cut over to 6th, a less crowded avenue and better for taking time to people-watch.

One evening I was on my way to school when I realized I had left a paper upstairs. I raced back into the building, right past the guards and straight into the private elevator of William Paley, CBS chairman. Mr. Paley himself was in the elevator, and I caught my breath. He was amused, and asked why I was in such a hurry. "I'm on my way to NYU," I squeaked, "and I left my critique upstairs and I'm going to be late, so . . ." "I'll give you a lift," he said. He waited until I got my paper, and we walked out together, past the befuddled guards. It was the first time I had ever ridden in a limousine, and I still remember its luxuriant, plush carpeting.

He asked me what I was studying, what I wanted to do, what my impression of CBS was. I was conscious of stammering throughout the entire ride. I thought how kind and attractive he was, but he seemed preoccupied and rather sad. I knew nothing about him other than the industry legends, and when I finally read his autobiography I realized this was the time his late wife Babe Paley was ill with cancer.

That was my only contact with Mr. Paley. He was a name out of a textbook, a historic figure in broadcasting. An amazing aspect of the industry is that it is so young that many of its pioneers are still working in it. Recently I attended an awards dinner given by the Cameraman's Association, and among those honored was Vladimir Zworykin, inventor of the iconoscope-kinescope tubes. There he was, well past ninety years old, the acknowledged Father of Television, still working in the business he all but invented.

I tried not to take my job as a personal insult. I kept reminding myself that I was only biding time, strengthening my experience and thus my resumé. On the other hand, it was dispiriting to have to put up with people who thought I was just a starry-eyed little girl. Men would say, "What are you knocking yourself out for? You'll end up getting married and having babies. *Relax.*" I could feel my face harden and I would have to divert my eyes before the anger percolating inside boiled over.

Happily, while I was working as a gofer at WCBS radio, I met several men who hadn't fallen victim to these chauvinistic clichés. If I arrived at the studio before 6 A.M., Charles Osgood, anchorman for the *Six to Nine Show*, let me sit with him while he wrote copy. I read over what he wrote, and, although the style was uniquely Osgood's, I was gradually able to assimilate something of his writing technique: how to knock out concise, clear, punchy news copy. I practiced writing, then practiced picking up speed. I learned to read three wire service versions of a story and cull them down, shaping them into my own style. I could relate the journalistic basics—who, what, why, when, where—of all the major stories on any given day. Radio and television news is necessarily simplistic, but good newscasters know—and communicate to the audience that they know—far more than the ten or twenty seconds' worth they read for each story. Charles was a patient tutor, looking over what I had written and suggesting how it could be improved. He gave me a lot of valuable pointers: Shorter is always better; a sentence that reads well might not speak well; sometimes a perfectly constructed sentence will have four esses in a row; think it out in your mouth; write for the audience's ear. Later in the day I might take my copy to Joe Dembo, the general manager, or Marv Friedman, the news director, and *they* would look it over.

It was probably Ed Bradley, now of *60 Minutes,* but then a WCBS radio reporter, who gave me the most consistent support. He had worked in Philadelphia at WDAS, a black-owned and operated station where he spun records and read news just as I had done in Rochester. Ed is a superb journalist, and was large-hearted enough to let me tag along with him from time to time when he covered a story. Although he got his job during the period of hiring token blacks, he was never a token. His capacity to disregard criticism—however covert—was remarkable. "You know who you are and what you can do," he used to say to me. "What difference does it make what anybody thinks?" We were in a sense kindred spirits struggling to make our way in an industry that was still largely a bastion of white males. He went on to do freelance reporting in Paris and then to cover Vietnam for CBS.

After I moved on to Texas, Ed sent me a copy of his first stand-up, and I wrote back telling him of an ingenious technique I had picked up: I pre-recorded my news stories on cassettes, and played them back through a concealed earphone while I repeated them aloud on air—staying a word or two behind the tapes. Not everyone can master this minor art of limiting "blown" on-camera stand-up reports. It is a little like patting your head and rubbing your stomach at the same time, but when you're working in combat or other dangerous situations, or when a tight news budget precludes footage enough for "Take Two," the technique can be a literal or figurative lifesaver.

As determined as we both were, we could never have guessed at the success that was to come. Certainly, as Eva Duarte was to say in the Broadway play *Evita*, we had "all the disadvantages necessary for success."

The head of the CBS Radio Group was Ed Joyce, a country gentry type with his pipe and tweedy, patched-elbow look. He had two nicknames at CBS: The Squire and The Velvet Scythe. The story around the network was that when he was going to take you apart, he was always soft-spoken, calm, and courteous. You left his office with a jaunty step until you remembered that you had just left your guts in there. I had been interviewed by Ed for a desk assistant's job, which he gave to someone else. Years later, when I was in talks with the various networks, I had lunch with Ed and Jim Cusick, a news writer and editor I had known at WCBS who was now a news director. They were offering me a position at the CBS flagship station in New York. All this time I had been nursing a desire to make a triumphant return to CBS, one of those childish instincts that propel you to "show them." (I remember an interview I did with Janis Joplin in Texas. She was from Port

Arthur, and all her life she had been an outcast, called sow and pig and other unspeakable names by kids who taunted her about her looks. After she became one of the most famous stars in rock history, she went back to Port Arthur in a blaze of glory to give a concert. "I came back for one reason, honey," she told me. "I want to jam it up their asses.") At last I had my chance to "show" Ed Joyce.

Over lunch I asked him: "*Why* didn't you hire me?" He studied his plate, arranged his tie, clasped his hands.

"You want the truth?" he answered.

"Please."

"Jessica . . . I—don't—even—remember—you."

That, as they say, put me in my place. The truth was, I didn't so much want to *show* Ed Joyce as to *impress* him. Recently made the number two executive vice president of CBS, Ed ranks among the finest of talents in the industry. He believes in the traditional precepts of journalism without ever being stodgy and lackluster. Many of the older correspondents seem to believe that if one is not grounded in print reporting, one is not a true journalist. Print reporters sometimes regard broadcasters as overpaid prima donnas. Broadcasters, on the other hand, tend to view print reporters as pedantic pencil pushers. Television journalism is such a new industry that when looking for skilled reporters, until recently it could only draw from print journalism. In truth, print and broadcast journalism are separate means to achieving the common end of informing the public. They each involve unique skills; one is neither a prerequisite for, nor superior to, the other. Now there is a new generation of correspondents, producers, and other personnel trained from the outset as broadcasters.

Well over a year passed and I was growing discouraged. It was obvious CBS was not going to give me a shot at reporting, and I had learned all the skills possible in my present position. Joan finally coerced WCBS-TV into making an audition tape of me reading the news, so I could try smaller markets in other parts of the country.

I worked on my script for three weeks, and asked Ed Bradley to watch me rehearse. We used a tape library at WCBS radio on a Saturday morning. "It looks like you're just trying to get through it," Ed cautioned me after I read my copy. "*Think* about what you're saying." That happens to be one of the major rules—or should be—in communications. Newscasters have an obligation to understand as thoroughly as possible everything they are trying to communicate to viewers.

I was given two copies of my tape, not the small, Betamax cassettes of today, but huge, high-band dubs in steel containers easily weighing ten pounds. I still have a copy of that audition, which

I have watched twice since—and both times I've cried. It was just terrible. You can see a man with clapsticks come out and say, "Savitch, take one," and you can see me in the background, so eager and so terrified, take a big gulp before I begin to read my script. I used to think the people who viewed my tape were dummies for not hiring me; I now suspect they showed good sense.

I sent letters to every news director in America in a market large enough to have the three network affiliated or owned and operated stations, noting that an audition tape was available on request. I got back six mimeo replies, two or three personal rejections, and a couple of requests for the tape.

Joel Chaseman, head of the Westinghouse stations, was one who generously agreed to see me. I walked over to his Park Avenue office on my lunch hour, dragging my ten-pound high-band dub. We watched the tape together, me solemn but hopeful beside him. When it was over he turned the lights on, looked at me wincingly, and said, "That was really horrible." I felt the muscles in my neck constrict. "However," he hurried to add, "you do have a definite presence on screen. If you work on your delivery, I predict you'll make a name for yourself one of these days." He gave me leads at a couple of Westinghouse stations, but as usual to no avail. Neither had a job opening.

By now I was desperate. This was 1970, the year of Nixon's wage-price freeze, and CBS was lopping people off its staff left and right. I knew my days were numbered. And then, at long last, I got an interview for an on-air reporting job with KHOU-TV, Channel 11, in Houston.

Chapter
6

On a sweltering Friday in May, I arrived in Houston wearing my only good suit, which was suede. Waiting to pick me up was the news director and anchorman at the station, Dick John, a cherubic-looking man with a beguiling twinkle in his eyes. His car was parked in the airport's circular garage, and as we drove down, my stomach began to churn. The flight had been unusually bumpy; I was hot and queasy with nerves. "Mr. John," I whispered, "I'm afraid I'm going to be sick." He found a ladies' room and I barely made it in before I threw up. Never had I been so humiliated. When I opened the door, Dick John was stationed outside with a handkerchief, but he pretended to ignore the incident. We drove on to

KHOU, along a vast and barren stretch of land. As we neared the city, I saw a building with an enormous Gulf sign, and I suppose it is a fair measure of my callowness that I assumed that it was a gas station for helicopters. Texas had been preceded by legends of preposterous bigness, so why not?

The station was about ten minutes from downtown Houston, on Allen Parkway—one of those labyrinthian arteries that looks, from on high, like a plate of spaghetti. I was introduced to the station manager, Dean Borba, who asked me a few questions about my background. Although Dick John was ultimately doing the hiring, Dean was giving his stamp of approval. I am still unsure why Dick hired me. He has been quoted in *Newsweek* as saying he knew star material when he saw it. I say he knew desperation.

I guess my timing, as they say, was right. Channel 11 was looking for two new reporters because the half-hour news was to be expanded to an hour in the fall. The FCC had ruled that networks should turn back half an hour of prime time television to local stations, the theory being that there should be more locally originated programs reflective of the community. Most local stations had nothing to fill the slot, so they simply stretched out the news. I was helped by that new law, but not by being female. My entry into Houston broadcasting predated by more than two years the feverish push to hire white women. Being female in 1970 still meant getting a job in spite of, not because of, being a woman. Not until an FCC mandate declared the female fifty-three percent of the population a *minority* did TV stations rush to hire women.

I returned to New York that evening, and the following Monday Dick called and offered me the job at a beginning salary of $135 a week. My rapture instantaneously turned to dismay when I realized that I would actually be moving to Houston. This was the old diamond-in-the-rough Houston, an overgrown cowboy town, not the sophisticated international metropolis it is today. I thought I was going to the middle of nowhere: The flat terrain, the scorching climate, the down-home gusto, the twangy drawl, everything was foreign to me. After a while I could appreciate the comic aspects of Texas—grocery chains called Piggly Wiggly, annual festivities called the Amarillo Armadillo Race and the Luling Watermelon Thump, the rich gallery of characters. But I was slow to abandon my eastern reserve, and for a long time I hadn't one friend.

I stayed temporarily at the Ramada Inn, waiting for my furniture to follow. The least expensive way I could move my belongings was in a communal truckload which was to make several stops in places like Kansas City and Texarkana before moseying on down to Houston. I would leave my motel room in the morning, and before I reached my car I had broken out in a profuse sweat from the tropical heat. Anyone who had heard I got the job on the basis of looks was quickly reassured by one glimpse of me with my hair in damp strings and my rouge running in rivulets down my face. In the evenings I ordered room service, or stopped off at Taco Bell or Church's Fried Chicken for take-out food.

———————— • ————————

Dick John drove me around to look at apartment buildings near the station. I spotted a quasi-high rise that looked pretty decent, particularly compared to New York. I thought it might be worth looking into. Dick let out a whoop. "Christ, Jessica, those are the *projects!*" The prototypical Houstonian apartment was motel-modern, fully furnished in your basic color schemes of orange-gold carpet and a harvest wheat refrigerator-stove combination, or avocado with olive drab accessories. For $169 a month I rented a clean, well-lighted, one-bedroom apartment with washer, dryer, dishwasher, garbage disposal, and air conditioner. Suddenly I was on top of the world.

What I omitted to tell Dick when he interviewed me was that I didn't know how to cover a story for television except in theory. I had the elementary journalistic skills but no on-air experience. "Maybe I ought to just go around with some of the other reporters to see if you do anything different here," I said to him my first day, and either he fell for the ploy, or he recognized the wisdom of it. "What a great idea," he said.

I was sent out with a cameraman named Bob Wolf, a big, burly waggish fellow who opened every conversation with every newcomer with the same droll comment: "I was here when you got here, and I'll be here when you're gone. So don't gimme no trouble." Bob had been Dan Rather's cameraman during Hurricane Carla, which made Dan's career and this was the second thing Bob let you know. Bob never took freeways—he'd been there before they were built, and he'd be there when they were gone, I reckon. He knew every byway, back alley and cul-de-sac in Houston. He always went to stories by crazy circuitous routes, but he always seemed to get there first.

"Let's go on over to the fuzz factory," he told me. I hadn't a clue what a factory for fuzz was. It turned out, of course, to be the police station. The

Houston police were a very tough force, long on law and order in the old-fashioned Texas frontier sort of way. Bob made his living by sitting at the fuzz factory waiting to go out with them to cover murders, drug raids, car crashes—any human drama that was newsworthy. Characters and crisis were the hallmarks of Houston news. News is what happens when individuals act, interact, and react. Houstonians did all three in a bigger-than-life way.

He drove me over to introduce me to "the boys," who were slack-jawed and incredulous. Female reporters were as yet a novelty, and the reactions I got ranged from laughable to galling. Typical was the phone call I took my first week in the newsroom.

"May I speak to a reporter?" a male voice asked.

"You're speaking to a reporter."

"No, I mean a *real* reporter."

"I *am* a reporter."

"Honey, put one of the fellows on, please." Naturally he thought I was the receptionist or secretary.

The police issued me a press card, and Bob and I returned to his car. Coming over his CB radio was some squawky static.

"Well, we got one," he drawled.

"One what?"

"A floater."

"Oh, good."

Once again, I had no idea what he was talking about. We drove over to the Houston Ship Channel and I saw the police near the water's edge. As we approached them, I was shocked to see they were putting a body in a bag—a decomposing body, to be precise, one of life's most wretched sights. The nearest I had come to a dead being was the fetal pig I dissected in biology class. The grotesquerie of the floater, the sharp oily stench of the channel, the violent midday sun, made my head spin. But I suspected that the manner in which I reacted would set the tone for the rest of my career in Houston. If I behaved like a sniveling kid, I might never be taken seriously back at the newsroom. Every few seconds Bob looked over his shoulder to check me out, but I watched him film the entire proceedings with swashbuckling bravado. Not once did I flinch, and when I got back to the car, I thought, "Well, I guess I've made it: I'm a reporter."

Over the long stretch, that kind of stoic resolve can harden into matter-of-factness. Later on in my Houston career, I was sent to cover a bank robbery which was still in progress. It was the third time this particular bank had been hit. During the second robbery, the bank manager had shot one of the robbers, and this time a bank employee had been killed in the shootout. We arrived minutes after it was over, police still ringing the building. I called the desk to tell them we didn't make it.

"Check it out to see if the corpse was that bank manager who shot the robber last time," I was told. I said we might not know anything for at least an hour, because the coroner had to make a positive identification. "The bank manager had a harelip," my assignment editor remembered. "If this man's got a harelip, we'll know it's him. We can get the jump on the story." I waited until the coroner arrived, then followed him to the back of the bank. He pulled the sheet back from the body; the man had taken a bullet right in the face. I wouldn't have known if he had had any lips, period.

"Damn!" I said to myself. "That kills *that* story. And I waited an hour and a half." As I was walking back to the parking lot, it hit me just how hard I had become. This poor man probably had left a wife and children, and all I could think was that I had wasted an hour and a half. Incontestably, a journalist must maintain some emotional distance, but you needn't be callous.

———— • ————

There is a syndrome in the industry I call Bad News-Good News: The bad news is that fifty people died in a hotel fire; the good news is that we got exclusive footage. How is a reporter supposed to feel about such an ambiguity? As a human, you react to the overwhelming tragedy of it. On the other hand, the reporter's job is to inform and disseminate news in a competitive field, to bring an accurate account to the public as quickly as possible. It is that duality that makes my job so tough, not knowing whether to cry or applaud.

Unfortunately, the industry moves and changes so fast in its technology, that we tend to put technological skills into play without really sitting down to reflect upon the ethical and moral ramifications. We've opened up new doors without fully understanding where they lead. Do we put the footage of the plane crash on immediately, before the relatives have been notified? How far should we go in reporting a disaster? How graphic should the story be, and how intimately should it be told? What is the value of sticking a microphone in a man's face right after he has learned of his wife's death?

I was sent to interview a woman who had just lost her family, and I couldn't bring myself to knock on her door. I did a stand-up on the lawn, and ended by saying "I would ask her how she feels, but I would imagine you know." The concept of telling a story in a personal way is a reasonable one, but too often it breaks down in the execution, going beyond the original point and lapsing into bad taste. Treading the fine line between creating empathy and invading someone's privacy is precarious, at best.

Our free enterprise system of disseminating information is collectively referred to as The Media. But there is no collective. There is no T*H*E*M*E*D*I*A, as in "The media has been attacking the president's economic policy," or "The media is lax in its coverage of big business." No club called The Media meets on alternate Thursdays to decide how it will or will not cover a given event, policy, institution, or individual. Instead of The Media covering a story, what really happens is individual reporters, trained to excerpt the salient points of a story, put them into a logical order and make decisions independent of any other reporter. There are enough reporters involved in this process that the viewer has a choice of whose coverage he or she will watch. The more choices, the better the coverage. The better the coverage, the more discriminating the viewer.

———— • ————

When you're on the scene of a story, you are inexorably involved not only intellectually and emotionally, but physically as well. I knew there were dangers inherent in my work, but I had the feeling that the doctor doesn't get sick, the lawyer doesn't get sued, and the reporter doesn't get hurt covering a story. A press card, I found out, does not provide you with an invisible shield. You're flesh and blood. You can as easily die racing to cover a bank robbery as you can in a war zone.

Two years ago I wrote a commentary on the subject when Bill Loomer, a cameraman who had worked with me covering fires and floods and shootouts in Philadelphia, died filming an innocuous jogathon. His helicopter hit a power line and catapulted into the river.

By far my most perilous assignment was covering a tank car explosion. I was driving along with cameraman Don Benskin, who had been one of Channel 11's most vocal opponents of going into the field with a woman. We were out on a routine assignment when suddenly we saw a huge, mushroom-shaped fireball on McKawa Road, near the Santa Fe Railroad tracks. I called in to the desk and the cameraman was stuck with me. It was a big story, and he knew it. As we sped toward the scene, he clenched his jaw in stony silence.

"I think our game plan should be . . ." I began.

"I think our game plan should be that you stay in the car," he interrupted.

I fought back my anger. "You take the sound gear," I said. "I'll shoot silent with the Bell and Howell and roll wild sound on my tape recorder. I'll hook up with you for the interviews and on-camera inserts."

"You're on your own, Savitch," he said.

All the area news people converged at once,

having gotten word that a train derailed. Eight cars were filled with an explosive chemical, and one had already blown up into a raging, immense fire. Residents who lived along the railroad track were being evacuated as firemen sprayed their houses.

We decided things looked stable enough to move back for an overview and on-camera insert. Just as I said, "Ok, roll," I saw his face turn stark white. "Run!" he screamed. Then I felt the boom. A second car had exploded, and flames roared monstrously toward the sky, singeing my eyebrows and turning my cheeks a bright, sunburnt red. We dropped our gear and threw ourselves into a ditch.

I remember the terrified screams and the panic as people rushed all around in a frenzy. In traumatized silence, not really understanding what was happening, we were held behind a police line until we could retrieve the cameras and tape recorder. In the meantime, word had gotten out that several firemen and news people had been killed. When at last we made it back to the newsroom, our colleagues rushed to embrace us, some of them crying. Thereafter, no one ever again said he didn't want to work with me.

Word came as I started to edit that the Cronkite show wanted a feed for the evening news. I watched Walter Cronkite at his desk holding his script, the trademark clicks sounding in the background. "CBS News with Walter Cronkite . . . click, click . . . Dan Rather at the White House . . . click, click, click . . . Jessica Savitch in Houston." Click. Making the Cronkite clicker gave me a status I in no way deserved at the time, but I was so upset about my colleagues who had been killed that I couldn't appreciate it.

———————— • ————————

I hadn't realized until I covered the police beat just how seedy crime is. The villain of the silver screen usually has a sinister, dashing sexuality, a picaresque appeal. Real criminals, more often than not, are swarthy, unkempt scoundrels. Shootouts are not gunfights of honor, they're gang wars and racial riots. I frequently had to remind myself that I was not just a spectator; I could easily become a protagonist.

There are times, of course, when you must be a protagonist of a different sort. In the aftermath of a Galveston hurricane, I flew by helicopter above the flooded streets, locking my feet under the pilot's seat as I held on to the cameraman's belt so he could lean out and film. When he was through shooting footage, we set about aiding in the rescue efforts. People were clinging to their roofs, and we were able to pull up two adults and a child.

Work of this nature involved long hours in close quarters and tough situations with male colleagues, most of whom were married. I have long counted it as important to meet the wives of these men with whom I work in sometimes intimate circumstances—such as all-night editing in small, dark rooms. (Bernice Kohler, wife of Philadelphia's KYW-TV film editor Allen Kohler, could joke that her husband was "spending the night with Jessica Savitch again.") Once when I was sent to cover another hurricane, I changed into foul weather gear on the side of the road and left some of my clothes in the back seat of cameraman Wally Athey's car. When a shocked Mrs. Athey found them that evening, she was relieved when her husband shrugged and said, "Oh, no problem, they're just Savitch's."

Weather stories could be particularly terrifying for me. Although one of the drawing points of Houston when I was offered the job was that I would be working at the same station where Dan Rather made a name for himself covering Hurricane Carla in 1961, I was eventually to learn that every reporter in the vicinity was looking to follow in Dan's footsteps. Every time an extra little bit of rain fell, we would all beg to do the story.

Texas newsrooms have hurricane reporting down to a science: the storm-coming-ashore story, the pre-disaster party, the evacuation, the homeless victims, the dig-out. When a hurricane was imminent, my first thought was how I could make history. My second thought was how I could get killed. I have had a lifelong phobia of snakes, and I knew that in a flood all living creatures—snakes included—will head for high ground. Every time I covered a storm I got excruciating pains extending from my waist all the way down to my heels. The pain took an average of three days to go away. My doctor was stymied. Did you fall, he asked, did you run, did you slip? No, no, no, I answered, but eventually we were able to pinpoint the symptoms. When I interviewed anyone in the aftermath—usually some macho guy who wouldn't come out of the water—I locked every muscle in my body for fear of water moccasins and rattlers slithering around me.

———— • ————

An especially brutal storm spawned by a hurricane devastated New Braunfels, a German-American city in the Texas hill country. When the river crested, it roared through town, making a clean sweep of nearly everything. Cameraman Ron Cutchall and I were dropped off by helicopter and left on our own. We arrived immediately after the height of the flood and helped in the rescue efforts while also shooting footage. It was a scene of wrenching horrors, of dazed and hysterical survivors whose every belonging had been destroyed. I talked to a man only minutes after he had watched his wife and baby daughter swept from his arms by the raging waters.

I got back to the station forty-five minutes before air time, streaked with mud and sweat, and used every available second writing and editing my story. Those were the days preceding portable videotape coverage; film came in 200- to 400-foot rolls called magazines, and required a minimum of half an hour to develop. I hadn't a moment to spare for the formality of doing my hair and makeup. I merely washed my face, gave my hair a hasty brushing and hurried to the studio. As I was leaving to go home after the newscast, proud of the job I had done, the switchboard operator stopped me. "Lawdy mercy, these phones have been ringing off the hook," she said. "You must have gotten about sixty calls already." I couldn't believe she was serious. Sixty calls was unheard of for a newscast in a market that size—usually it was one or two. "What in the world are they saying?" I asked her. "Aw honey, don't be too upset . . . but everybody says you looked awful." It was at that moment that I understood the delicate balance of looks and ability in television. It is, after all, a visual industry, and exterior packaging plays an incontrovertible role, although ultimately, of course, there has to be something of substance *inside* the package. Looks should neither attract nor distract. Ideally, a reporter's appearance should just be pleasant enough to be disregarded.

The question of looks, which inevitably comes up in interviews, is a consistently awkward one for me. It's one of those when-did-you-stop-beating-your-wife questions. If you affirm it, you're guilty; if you deny it, people think you're lying. If you're asked, "Do you think you would be where you are today if you weren't pretty?" and you answer honestly, "Looks are part and parcel of the industry," you have made a de facto admission that you think you're good-looking. On the other hand, if you're coy or try to skirt the issue, "Oh, I'm not really that attractive; I have a crooked tooth and a nose that's off-center and a square jaw," it looks as though you're fishing for compliments.

The minute viewers write or call in about your looks, it means they were not listening to what you were saying. If your looks distract from the story, then the process of communication is interrupted. I have decided to quit apologizing for my looks, which have played both a positive and negative role in my career. I have my own theory that attractive people in the industry are considered bad journalists; average looking reporters are automatically given more credence.

A fact of modern life is that it takes women longer to get ready than men. As NBC makeup artist Barbara Kelly once told me, all she has to do is take a swipe at John Chancellor's face with a powder puff as he runs to the studio and hope to miss his glasses. Few female newscasters can get away with just a powder puff. You have to allow for time to fix your face, particularly on the road when you can't rely on the speedy expertise of trained stylists like Alan D'Angerio and other NBC professionals; it's you and a set of hot rollers.

Trailing candidates during the 1980 presidential campaign, I had to have my bags packed and ready for pick-up outside my hotel room an hour and a half before we caught a flight to our next destination—often as early as 7 A.M. That meant I had to be up by 4:00 or 4:30 after a late night because I also had to be presentable for the camera. The news business is definitely tougher on women, but they are not allowed to say that. If you ask for help, you're being a demanding prima donna. ("Next she'll want Monsieur Marc and a litter with six Nubian slaves.") On the other hand, if your looks aren't up to standard, these critics will be the first to point it out. A male newscaster can wear the same dark suit with a change of neckties for several days running; if a woman wore the same dark dress, people would write and ask, "Why does she wear such boring clothes?"

When I was anchoring in Philadelphia, I had to elbow my way into a space at the first floor public lavatory mirror. Unfortunately, my pre-5:30 news cleanup coincided with the assembling of the audience for *The Mike Douglas Show,* taped in an adjoining studio. Every day, with just a few minutes to go before air time, I slapped on makeup and sprayed my hair at the washbasin—surrounded by a fascinated audience of women. As my friend Maury Levy of *Philadelphia Magazine*, now with *Playboy*, wrote, my primping sessions were "a bonus that came with the purchase of a Mike Douglas ticket." I begged for my own makeup mirror, but was denied on the basis that my co-anchors, males, had never asked for one. Finally one day I was bestowed with a blinding, bulb-festooned contraption so big that, depending on the angle you stood, it could give you third-degree burns.

I've heard stories about Barbara Walters insisting on taking a retinue of aides along on the road—in truth, probably her makeup artist, hair stylist, and secretary. The fact of the matter is that when the *Today Show* was filming in far-off locales, Barbara most likely had to deal with time changes, preparations for interviews and satellite feeds. She had to concentrate on the substance of the story, not the cosmetics.

There are also the rumors of Nancy Dickerson having sent crew members out to get lifts put on her shoes so she would be as tall as the male reporters on location. The implications are that she was too involved with her looks. I followed in the footsteps of both Barbara Walters and Nancy Dickerson at NBC. When I arrived I could almost hear the men thinking here's another one of these women; what does *she* expect? I don't expect star treatment, and I don't think Barbara Walters or Nancy Dickerson or Betty Furness or any other of the first female newscasters at NBC and elsewhere did either. Ultimately, we just want to do our jobs properly.

What does all this have to do with journalism? one might well ask. Nothing. It has to do with a visual industry. Newscasters cannot call attention to themselves by being too attractive or too unattractive. The goal is to appear pleasantly well-groomed so that viewers forget your looks.

Happily, the camera can hide newscasters' concessions to weather. I have seen Capitol Hill correspondents, shot from the waist up, do stand-ups in suit jackets, ties, and cut-offs. That is the beauty of being a disembodied head. One way Channel 11 shrunk its expenses was to reduce the air conditioning on weekends. Cutting down the air conditioning in Texas is like cutting off your oxygen supply on the moon. A Houston summer is one of nature's sadistic jokes; compound it with the relentlessly hot lights of the studio and it's slow torture. I got into the habit of wearing shorts and sandals in the newsroom, topped with a blazer and tailored blouse at air time. On my last show, after I said goodbye, two crew members sauntered over and lifted my desk away—thereby revealing the total woman, bare legs and all.

Chapter 7

Houston, as it happened, was a wonderful place for a young reporter to start. I had a succession of great stories with little executive interference. KHOU was then a station in what was a backwater market. With a shoestring budget, it had neither the technological sophistication nor the format of larger Eastern stations, so I was sent out as a one-woman crew. We relied heavily on the Cut 'n' Shoot technique—the video counterpart of Rip 'n' Read—reporters filming their own newsreels with a Bolex or Bell and Howell. We didn't do just one story a day, we did two, sometimes three, for which we wrote copy and edited film for the anchormen. Being simultaneously a reporter, field producer, camerawoman, writer, and editor soon taught me what can and cannot realistically be expected on a story. I quickly learned not to plan a scene around a technologically impossible shot. Today I am better able to articulate what I want in a shot, a skill generally appreciated by cameramen and women.

Texas was defined by its larger-than-life characters, particularly politicians. The electrically charged political arena was like a microcosm of national shenanigans right down to the scandals and the good-old-boy network of smoke-filled rooms. When the legislature was in session, I got up at sunrise, hopped a chartered plane as soon as it was light enough to take off, flew to Austin, and then returned by 4:00 in time to process my film and write my story.

The gubernatorial race of 1972, particularly the Democratic primary, was my first involvement with a major campaign. Covering such a race in a state as large as Texas is like covering a presidential campaign from Atlanta, Georgia, to Rockland, Maine.

The most memorable candidate was Frances "Sissy" Farenthold, a lawyer, state representative, and later head of the National Women's Political Caucus, who demonstrated to me that it is possible to be simultaneously aggressive and feminine. Sissy Farenthold was running for governor in a state known for its tough, two-fisted politics, and yet she pulled a significant number of delegates. Texas was big enough to accommodate the idea of women in political roles—the illustrious Barbara Jordan was already making news as a state senator and first female president pro tem of the state senate—and hints of the liberal Eastern influence that have made Houston the diverse city it is today were evident in the Farenthold victory in Harris County.

Her campaign plane, boasting a green-painted "SISSY" on the sides, was as out-dated as a covered wagon. We nicknamed it The Vomit Comet, inspired by its tendency to bounce turbulently even on a perfect day. The atmosphere on board was always lively, optimistic, and good-humored, men wearing buttons proclaiming, "I'm a male chauvinist pig for Sissy."

By contrast, the eventual Democratic nominee, millionaire landowner Dolph Briscoe, traveled sedately about in a sleek Learjet. Briscoe was a man of much political acumen but little zest, dubbed by a columnist "a bowl of political pablum." Despite that jibe, Briscoe served successfully as a two-term governor.

I loved every exhausting, amusing, fascinating moment of the campaign, except for one experience I hope never to repeat. A man named Ben Barnes, who also ran for the Democratic nomination in the primary, conceived of the clever publicity stunt of hiring a train to traverse Texas. For three days I joined his entourage on this old-fashioned whistle-stop tour, chugging from Amarillo in the panhandle to the Gulf, past endless cattle feed lots extending for miles into the sun-baked horizon.

At each stop, Ben Barnes waved enthusiastically to the local folks from the back car, à la Roosevelt, and each time regional specialties were brought aboard for us to eat. The fried chicken bits in Sweetwater, Texas, were especially delicious, I thought. "Tastes a lot like fried chicken, doesn't it?" remarked my cameraman, John Shaw. "It is fried chicken," I returned, my throat already instinctively constricting. "Isn't it?" "Aw, hell, no. Sweetwater's the home of the Rattlesnake Roundup. This here's rattlesnake filet." My nightmares of snakes wrapping their slimy lengths around my body was nothing compared to the horror of having them floating inside my stomach. That marked the second time I humiliated myself in front of my Houston colleagues by losing my lunch.

———— • ————

In the beginning, I found my height a handicap: Push comes to shove pretty often in this business. If I didn't push hard enough trying to work my way through a packed room to get to the speaker, a technique known in Houston as the gang-bang interview, I was shoved to the outside of the crowd.

At a rally that was staged for Senator Muskie during his campaign for the presidency, I competed with a multitude of other reporters to get close enough to ask a few questions for the evening newscast. I was stuck in the body-to-body mob several yards away from him until a rangy, broad-shouldered Texan, crying, "Why it's that cute li'l ole gal from Channel 11!," picked me up, literally held me above his head, and barreled his way through the throng. He deposited me directly in front of the senator. Triumphantly, I looked across the sea of faces to make sure my cameraman was rolling. He was waving something wildly back and forth. My heart sank. It was my disconnected microphone cable.

Usually at these big events the camera equipment was brought to location early, and the first person to arrive from any of the three stations— Channels 2, 13, or 11—had to light the set. Until I caught onto the gag, the crews from 2 and 13 hid, thus assuring that I was the person. Since I could not possibly lift three full cases at once, I had to lug them, up stairs, down halls, across rooms, two lights at a time. When I finished, sore and worn out, the men would appear to congratulate me, flashing their Cheshire grins.

———— • ————

My colleagues had great fun teasing me. I was assigned to do a story on a catfish farm near La Grange, Texas, and on my way out of the studio the assignment editor said to me, "By the way, there's some chicken ranch in La Grange that's supposed to be a big deal. Check it out and see if there's a story there and we can run them together." Catfish farming and chicken ranching, that seemed consistent enough. I wrote it down in my notebook. Crew members stood around, their faces impassive. When we got to La Grange, the cameraman said, "I know where the catfish farm is, but I don't know where that chicken ranch is. You're gonna have to ask." The rule of the road—unless you were involved in a car chase—was that the cameraman drove and the reporter followed the map or asked for directions. I got out of the car and walked over to a young man leaning against a storefront. "Pardon me, I need to go to the chicken ranch. Could you tell me how to get there?"

"The chicken ranch?! Whoa!" he said, slapping his thigh and laughing.

"What's the matter?" I demanded. "What's so funny?"

"Well, it ain't too often I get asked that question by a *lady*," he said. "Hoo boy!"

At that moment I saw that cameraman John Shaw was filming us. He was having me on, as the British say. The chicken ranch was a whorehouse—in fact, The Best Little Whorehouse in Texas.

We drove on to the farm, John ribbing me the whole way. He set up the camera, and let it roll. "First of all," I asked the farmer, "for all those people out there who don't know, how did catfish get their name?"

"'Cause they got whiskers," he said.

"Cut!" I yelled. "OK, that's enough, John. You've wasted enough footage with these stupid pranks!"

I wheeled on the farmer. "I'm aware he's put you up to this, but I don't think the people watching the news are going to appreciate your little joke."

The farmer was utterly dumbfounded.

"I don't know what your problem is, lady," he said, "but catfish has got *whiskers*."

I stared at the slick fish he had pulled from the water, at its wiry protuberances that looked exactly like a cat's whiskers—I was mortified. Still I figured that if I could be sent to a whorehouse to do a story on chickens, I could be told that fish need to shave.

———— • ————

The man who made The Best Little Whorehouse in Texas a national household word was Marvin Zindler, a Beau Brummell who favored patent leather shoes buffed to a brilliant luster and early mobster zoot suits. The first time I saw him, he was swanking down the halls of the fuzz factory. "Who is *that?*" I asked Bob Wolf. "Oh, some flack who works for the sheriff's office," he said. Apparently the sheriff's department and the police department had had a long-standing rivalry, so the sheriff created a public relations division under the guise of a consumer fraud unit.

What Marvin did was set up little media events for the three television stations. "Look," he would say when he called, "there's a grocer over here on the South Side who's been ripping off the public by jacking up the price of the produce. I'll be arresting him this afternoon at 3:00. That'll give you time to get your film processed for the 6:00 news." We would go down to the store, and Marvin would show up in all his dandified splendor to bust some poor cracker or Mexican-American— but not until he was sure the cameras were set up. "You got your lights ready Channel 11?" he would call out. "OK, Channel 2?" On a whim, I did a story on Marvin setting up the story: "Hey, Channel 13, I think you'd get a better shot over there by the door. All set? OK, lights!" I was not a favorite of Marvin's after that. He *hated* it. In any event, he went on to become the consumer reporter for

Channel 13, bringing overnight fame to the whorehouse when he busted it.

Like it or not, local newscasts are also part entertainment, and show biz played a leading role in Texas broadcasts. One of the most overused news entertainments in all of America is the Ringling-Brothers-Comes-to-Town story. Invariably local reporters are assigned to ride an elephant. It's free publicity for the circus, better than any advertising they can possibly buy, so they make the same preposterous story available every year to every local station in the country. And it works every damned time. I had vowed I was never going to get involved in the more embarrassing aspects of such coverage, like being forced to ride an elephant.

"Your assignment today is to ride the elephant," my news director said to me one steamy summer morning. I said I was not going to ride anybody's elephant on anybody's newscast *ever*. "I think it'll be good for your image," he countered. "It might soften it a little bit." If you're too hard, the theory goes, the audience won't like you. If you're too soft, they won't respect you. So you're expected to be sort of tough-vulnerable, or some amalgam thereof. "Besides," he added laconically, "you'll do it because I'm assigning you to do it."

I did it. I knew I would, even before I attempted my useless protest. The code of the newsroom is to never refuse an assignment except when there is a conflict of interest, a potential of danger to you or your family, or you hold a strongly biased attitude about the subject under focus. You can't say "I won't do the story." You *can* say, "I'll handle it my way."

In this case, I approached the story from the point of view of the poor elephant who, in town after town, has to lumber around the circus grounds with dippy reporters like me on his back while kids shove ice cream cones up his trunk. A silent camera was attached to my ankle, and I wrote an elephant's-eye view for the evening news, with a voice-over by the station's announcer. It was the closing story, and it got more phone calls than anything else on the newscast.

—————— • ——————

I was perhaps too insecure in the beginning, too quick to be defensive. Any day that I didn't get the lead story or the best story or beat the competition, I grew skittish and nervous. It meant to me that I was being discriminated against, or that I was not trusted. I was motivated by fear, more so than at any other point in my career. I lived with the constant terror that it would all be taken away, that the omnipotent they, whoever they may be, would come along, rip away my notebook, and boot me back into the street. When for so long you can't get a job for reasons that seem specious, when you finally do have it, you are constantly afraid of losing it for reasons you can't understand. In my terror of losing ground, I was overly intense, sometimes recklessly so, as when I covered the Abilene trial of House Speaker Gus Mutscher, who was convicted of bribery and conspiracy charges. A swarm of newspeople attempted to take still and motion pictures after the verdict, and in the scuffle a deputy sheriff shoved my cameraman. Impulsively, I hit him on the arm with my microphone, and it made all the local newspapers. Later that year I was actually arrested along with two other Houston reporters at the scene of an airline hijacking in Lake Jackson. The altercation stemmed from attempts by temporarily deputized citizens to prevent us from entering a private airport where the plane had landed. We kicked, and were charged with assault. "Free Jessica" bumper stickers briefly appeared following my arrest, but the charges were soon dropped. That kind of behavior was out of character for me, for I did not yet have the pliancy of self-assurance.

Chapter
8

Three months after I started at Channel 11, a notice went up on the bulletin board that auditions would be held for weekend anchor. I was so conditioned to thinking of anchoring as male turf that it hadn't even occurred to me to try out until Dick John persuaded me to consider it. The day I auditioned I pulled my hair back, wore a severely tailored blue suit, and gave my best male imitation for the camera. I had never seen a woman anchor the news, so I didn't know enough to just go on and behave like myself—I tried to look authoritative, and instead I looked silly.

Nonetheless, I got the job. The events of the following three months took at least three years for me to assimilate. In that short span I had gone from being Jessica Savitch who was inundated with rejections from Xerox machines all across America, to Jessica Savitch, first anchorwoman in the south. *TV Guide* and publications all over the South and West rushed in to do stories on me. I had never heard of reporters interviewing other reporters, and I felt clumsy on the other side of the notebook. Mail poured in by the sackload, more than anyone in Houston had ever received. "I've never been to Heaven," a local disc jockey sang, "but I've seen Jessica on Channel 11."

Suddenly being recognized on television meant I was referred to as a "broadcasting star". It mystified me because I still saw the same face in the mirror every morning. What did I have today that I didn't have three months ago? How long would it last? All I wanted was to be the best reporter, do the best interview, get the best footage. My goal was to be a network correspondent by the time I was thirty, and I figured that, at the pinnacle of my career, I would be lucky to make $30,000. I did not yet know that the industry was changing so fast that six-figure anchors would be at the top of the ladder.

The idea of stardom, both unexpected and instant, was difficult to grasp. To be more precise, I was uneasy with recognizability. It was like being schizophrenic: There was *her*, the woman on television, and *me*—the real me. I quit going to restaurants and to parties. Walking into a room filled with people you don't know who know *you* brings out your worst vulnerabilities. They would say things about me out loud as though I were still behind the screen—usually, "Oh, she's so much smaller than she looks on television!" No matter what your size, your shoulders fill up the screen just as a man's do. In person, I was less than the viewers imagined. I sensed the palpable disappointment people often have when they see a well-known person in the flesh, a someone like themselves who is not larger than life.

Recognizability is not necessarily a barometer of your skills or worth; it may simply mean that your face and name are known. I think of Paddy Chayefsky's movie, *Network*. There is anchorman Howard Beale being called into the office of a television executive who proselytized about capitalism, insisting Howard should be the harbinger of this great message. Imbued with his messianic importance, Howard asks, "Why me?" Simple, the executive explained: "Because you're on television, dummy." That year in its Christmas catalogue, Nieman Marcus advertised life-sized dummies you could have made of yourself, and I was astonished to discover the store had produced a replica of *me*. Why me? I was stunned but immensely flattered until I faced the inevitable reason. I rated the dummy not because of who I was or what I was, but because I was on television.

In my lowly days at CBS, I sometimes spent my lunch hour wandering through Bloomingdale's,

which one year decorated rooms to suit the personalities of certain celebrities. I walked about,
eating a hot dog from a street stand and was
yelled at for dripping mustard on the "Craig
Claiborne" carpet. Several years later, in my third
year as an anchor in Philadelphia, I was shocked
to learn that the local Bloomingdale's had decorated a Jessica Savitch room.

I worked half my life to be an overnight success,
and still it took me by surprise. Long past the
point when I should have felt comfortable in my
career, I had not yet accepted my success. Though
my recognizability is in no way comparable, I can
understand why superstars—Janis Joplin, Jimi
Hendrix, Jim Morrison, Lenny Bruce, Marilyn
Monroe, Elvis Presley, Freddie Prinze are just a
few names off the top of my head—burn out. I've
no doubt that John Belushi, too, was a victim of
his own bewildering achievements.

John's dressing room was next door to mine
when I did the news on the eighth floor at NBC.
One Saturday night, after I finished *Update* at
10:00, I ran into him on his way to dress rehearsal
in his Samurai outfit. "Samurai attack!" he yelled,
picking me up and depositing me in his dressing
room. Every time I tried to bolt for the door, he
drew his sword. He finally permitted me to escape, and he returned to the frenetic pace of his
rapidly escalating career, and what was later described as a disintegrating personal life. Although

a brilliant performer, John really *was* a Not Ready
for Prime Time Player; but who *is* ready for the
sudden seesaw of stardom, not being able to separate your own worth from your public persona?

Recognizability has its fillips, such as free bowls
of fruit in your hotel room and an extra drink at
the bar, but along with all the kudos go the risks,
the life-threatening moments. Few people in this
business like to talk about their close encounters
with the Mark Chapmans of the world, because to
do so risks stimulating them.

Shortly after my marriage to Don Payne one of
the most terrifying experiences of my life was reported in the *New York Post* under the headline
"TV Girl in Latest Reagan Scare." (Despite my
thirty-three years, I was still qualified to be described as a news girl. One cannot help but wonder if, at the same age, Roger Mudd or John
Chancellor was known as a newsboy.) Soon after
the Hinckley assassination attempt on President
Reagan, I received a letter from a deranged ad-
mirer who threatened to kill Vice President Bush
and Secretary of State Haig. I was filling in on the
Today Show, and early one morning, alone in my
office, I heard a voice behind me say, "Are you
Jessica Savitch?" I turned around and saw a nicely
dressed young man of about twenty-five staring at
me with a strange, haunted look. "I just want to
see you," he went on. "Talk to you . . . touch you."

I lunged toward him, pushing him backward,

and slamming the door. I bolted it shut and, in a panic, called Marty Wall, a former treasury agent who heads the security department. In the meantime, the man escaped. Because he had identified himself as the same person who had signed the letter of death threats, I spent the afternoon with the Justice Department and the local police. Apparently he was able to circumvent NBC security (it has since been considerably tightened), but he was captured almost immediately and consequently jailed. But the terror I experienced took its tragic toll: Although fully understanding that risks of this nature go with the territory, I can never again be blithely, comfortably unaware of the inherent danger of the job.

We have a way of building up heroes in this country, and then—sometimes by design, sometimes by default—tearing them down. Robert Altman illustrated this in *Nashville*, I think. The singer, supposedly based on Loretta Lynn, was promoted, hyped, used, abused, and propelled into stardom—only to have it all end when she was shot down on stage by some crazed kid who felt jilted or wanted some of the recognition himself. But we don't just shoot our heroes; we often destroy them by setting up unrealistic expectations. Fans want stars to "be who you are in our fantasies." Celebrities are made vulnerable when they begin to believe they are valued for themselves and not for what they do, when they begin to believe the power is theirs to keep and not just on loan.

A magazine cartoon I saw recently depicted a father and son watching a square-jawed anchor on television with a caption reading, "Yes, son, in this great country of ours, you, too, could grow up to be a TV anchorman." Newscasters have become latter-day electronic heroes.

When our news team in Philadelphia soared from number three to number one, the station did a promotion called "Learning to Live with Success," a comic before-and-after. It began with a vignette showing us sitting in our former obscurity in a restaurant, unable even to capture the attention of the waitress. "After" had us besieged by waitresses and patrons, piling food on our table and begging for autographs. Later that week, silk screen T-shirts with our pictures and names and "Learning to Live with Success" were distributed about town; placards went up on buses with our larger-than-life images. I would be walking down the street and suddenly see my own face staring back at me.

The jealous guarding of privacy takes on exaggerated emphasis when strangers pull up chairs and join you and your date in restaurants (one man brought along his toast for me to sign) as though you belong to them. And to a degree you do: Inescapably, part of your life is lived in public.

It took five or six years, long after I left

Houston, for me to fully accept that that mass recognizability meant that I would be described as a "star," and to be able to mellow out. Just over a year ago I was on the walkway in front of my townhouse in Washington, wearing baggy jeans, a babushka, and no makeup. A neighbor came out and introduced herself. "It's nice to meet you," I said. "I'm Jessica Savitch." "Jessica Savitch? *The* Jessica Savitch?" she asked, totally taken aback. And before she could stop herself, she blurted out, "But you look like an ordinary person!" Then she stammered, "I didn't mean . . . you know what I mean . . ." "It's all right," I smiled. "I *do* know what you mean."

Chapter
9

I stayed in Houston two years, and as I look back on it, I think I was perhaps in too big a hurry to get out. There was still a lot more to learn, but I knew that to move up was to move out. I was young and energetic and restless, filled with the urgency of my ideals.

Much of what I believed about my mission in the industry was formulated with a fellow Houston reporter named Ron Kershaw. We saw ourselves as innovative reporters in an emerging field. No one better embodies broadcast journalism than Ron, who has the greatest instinctual gift for what makes good news of anybody I have met in the business. He managed to strike a balance between the best parts of show business and the ethics of journalism, and he taught me a lot about how television is more than just a radio story with some pictures added.

Ron was my first serious romance. He was a reporter for KTRK-TV and we met when we were sent to cover a strike at an underground leftist radio station called KPFT. Although I had seen him many times on air—and in fact considered him the best reporter in the city—I had not really noticed how attractive he was. Going up the ragtag stairwell to KPFT, he caught my eye at the exact moment I caught his. He invited me to a Yes concert that weekend, and I was to say yes to Ron for years to come: We fell in love.

I accepted an offer from a Westinghouse broadcast station, KYW-TV, Channel 3, in Philadelphia, the fourth largest market in the country, covering a tri-state area: Southeastern Pennsylvania, all of Delaware, and some of New Jersey. In November of 1972, I packed my bags and headed east, so ambivalent about what I had done that it took me five days to make the trip. Two days for the actual drive to Philadelphia, three days worth of U-turns while I kept changing my mind about leaving Houston.

Ron was promised a job with Philadelphia's WPVI-TV, Channel 6, owned by Capitol Cities Broadcasting, the same station that owned KTRK in Houston. He was to follow me after the first of the year. We became engaged on Christmas Day and planned a spring wedding. But when KTRK found out he was to marry "that girl over at Channel 3," they promptly rescinded the job offer, saying they didn't want their reporter "in bed with the competition." We approached my new employer to offer ourselves as a kind of package deal, but KYW refused. They, too, wanted nothing to do with a newsroom marriage. (Today, such husband-wife teams as Chris Curle and Don Farmer of Cable News Network are common.)

Ron was eventually hired by WBAL-TV in Baltimore, a Hearst station which had as its chief competitor WJZ-TV, like KYW, a Westinghouse station. He took a job as news producer, rapidly rising to news director. Concomitantly, WBAL's ratings rose, topping WJZ's by several share points. The higher the rating, the larger the amount of money the commercials bring in. So, while Westinghouse saved a few dollars by not hiring Ron at KYW in Philadelphia, it lost millions in advertising revenues in Baltimore as WJZ continued to lose out to Ron's newscast at WBAL.

Our romance was on and off for years, affected by our work and the geographical distance. There were a lot of good times but also a lot of times when we drifted apart. His being in the business did not make him more understanding of the pressures of my job. Ron was a sympathetic supporter of women in the industry. He hired future major-market anchorwomen, such as Sue Simmons in New York and Amanda Arnold in Houston, as well as producers like Sharon Sakson, now with ABC, and Jennifer Siebens of CBS. Despite that, Ron had difficulty accepting the pressures of my job, and I developed little patience for his. He could handle the idea of Jessica the news reporter, but not Jessica the news reporter who was his girlfriend. My career took off, and my double bind was that I wanted to succeed while also wanting to make Ron happy. I can remember hiding the first magazine article written about me, tossing it under the shoes in my closet before Ron arrived for the weekend.

Women of my generation were brought up to believe that it was unfeminine to work and to be assertive, and men brought up to believe that a man should take care of the woman. All of a sudden, the rules changed on us—and we didn't know what to do. In the end we broke our engagement. Today Ron is a successful executive at NBC Sports, his office only a few floors away from mine.

———— • ————

Although I was hired by KYW to be a general assignment reporter and weekend anchor, I was told that I would likely be replacing Marciarose

Shestack—the first anchorwoman in the country—on the noon news. Marciarose had the dubious distinction of being told by a news manager that "A woman will anchor here over my dead body." He survived. She prevailed and is still working as a well-respected television journalist. At the time I arrived in Philadelphia, Marciarose had taken a leave of absence to work with the McGovern-Shriver campaign and was not expected to return.

On my first day, I sat down next to a congenial black woman named Bobbie Craddock. We introduced ourselves, and she told me she had just been hired away from her job as a general assignment reporter in Cleveland. "Right now I'm the consumer reporter," she said. "But the woman who does the noon news has taken a leave of absence and it looks like she won't be coming back. They've promised me her job if she doesn't." I gasped. What KYW had done was bring two women in to replace another woman, told the first woman her job would be there if she wanted to come back, and pitted the two newcomers against each other. They lied to Bobbie, they lied to me, they lied to Marciarose, and they left us to fight it out the best way we could. Marciarose returned to the station to host a new interview program. Bobbie Craddock resigned and found work in New Orleans. I was named anchorwoman. Ultimately, I suppose that meant I won. Somehow, I was never very happy about it.

Discrimination and dishonesty are never good business. They're no longer expedient in an industry that has to turn a profit. Tom Pettit, executive vice president of NBC News, tells the story of the scorpion and the camel. A flood has ravaged a region of the Middle East and the camel is preparing to swim across to dry land. "Take me with you," implores the scorpion. "Do you think I'm nuts?" says the camel. "If you sting me, I'll drown." "Do you think I'm *stupid*?" says the scorpion. "If you drown, I'll drown too." That's logical, thinks the camel. "Very well, climb on." Midriver, the scorpion stings him. As the camel is going down, he turns around and asks, "Why?" "What can I say?" shrugs the scorpion. "That's the Middle East for you." It's also the news business. That story sums up the working of men and women in this industry and in others. It is so competitive now that if time is wasted on the sting of dishonesty and discrimination within a news shop, it takes away from the energy needed to fight the flood of competition.

Perhaps the old male claim that woman had little camaraderie had its basis in truth: They were set up for rivalry. I am often asked if I'm the new Barbara Walters, and I always say, "The last I heard, the so-called old Barbara Walters is alive and well and doing a great job at ABC." And it always puts me in mind of those days when there was room for only one woman in the newsroom.

If a new one came in, that meant the old one was leaving. I was probably one of the few women in the industry to have a female mentor. Afterwards, I asked Joan Showalter what I could do for *her*, since she had done so much for me. Pass it on, was what she told me; dispel the myth that women are threatened by other women, that they won't help each other.

———— • ————

When KYW offered me the job, they insisted on a five-year contract. After I deliberated about it, I decided that five years was excessive. It was a mere formality, I was assured. If ever I wanted to leave there would be no problem, I would be released.

Over the next two years I became increasingly disgruntled. I was doing well as weekend anchor, and yet when the need arose to use substitutes on prime time nightly news, I was ignored. One of two male reporters was consistently chosen to fill in when the anchors were on vacation. Traditionally, weekend anchors fill in on prime time, and top-level reporters in turn fill in on weekends. They were also considering pairing me with someone on the weekend news who was not journalistically sound, as far as I was concerned. Then

CBS dangled the possibility of a job offer in front of me.

Reminding the administrative powers of their promise of release, I gave two weeks' notice—whereupon I was slapped with an injunction and a back-to-work order. In addition, not knowing with which network I was talking, the station wrote to all three networks, saying, "We advise that if you are in negotiation with Jessica Savitch, she is under binding contract to us." ABC and NBC might well have had no idea who I was, but they certainly took a look after they received these mysterious letters. It was the best publicity KYW could possibly have given me. If tested, many contracts in the industry would probably be proven unconstitutional, because there is no mutuality when an individual promises five years out of a career in return for a corporate guarantee of thirteen weeks' job security. Young people starting out are at a disadvantage: In order to beat the old axiom of no job without experience, no experience without a job, newcomers are often forced to sell out cheaply.

Sportscaster Warner Wolf, I am told, had a similar experience in Washington. He was not allowed to leave for the networks, and it is rumored that he was so angry he went on the air one night and said, "The scores today were 18, 23, 14, 26, 11, and 7. Back to you." Whether the fact of that story lives up to the legend is beside the point.

The examples of bad feelings and battered careers are numerous industry-wide. Although I was tempted to get out of the job by not showing up for work or by doing poorly, if nothing else, I owed it to myself and to the viewers to do my best. I actually had little choice but to go back. That, or exhaust my finances and emotions fighting a court battle that would likely continue past the date the contract would expire on its own. Gradually, however, it dawned on me that while the contract could require my staying, it could not make me perform any assignment to which I was not journalistically committed or for which I was not compensated comparably to male colleagues performing the same job functions. I went back to work and sweetly explained that they indeed held the contract, but I held the cards. Their choice was to aid me in my development, live up to the law of the land that called for equal pay for equal work— or fire me. I was made prime time co-anchor on the 5:30 and 11 P.M. newscasts at double my salary.

Even though I had won, I felt suffocated, closed in; I hyperventilated and lost my appetite. My weight dropped to an all-time low, and I hovered on the brink of malnutrition. I was tense, high-strung, and uncommunicative. Finally, something in me snapped. I knew that I could not continue this way. A friend, KYW Assignment Editor Dave Neal, gave me a framed quote that still hangs in my office: "Do what you can with what you have where you are." Theodore Roosevelt said that, and it served as my lodestar. I set about on an exhaustive campaign of self-improvement. I think of it now as a fast-action scene in a movie, meant to suggest the active passage of time, frames blinking nimbly into other frames. A well-known speech coach, Lillyan Wilder, helped me rid myself of the vestiges of a lateral lisp. Until I was well into my teens, I would call myself Jethica Thavitch. I worked on my on-camera presentation and my writing. I insisted on producing specials of substance. "Lady Law," a documentary on women and police work, won the Dupont-Columbia Award for best news feature.

The dilemma of women in police work paralleled what I had gone through with certain crew members in Texas. Nobody disputed that they were smart enough to go out on sector patrol, rather, that they weren't strong enough. Yet in order to ascend the ranks from sergeant to detective to captain to inspector, a police officer *had* to begin with patrol work. Philadelphia became the Justice Department's test case.

I entered the police academy with the first-class recruits, learning to fire a weapon and struggling through gruelling obstacle courses. Afterwards, my muscles were so stiff I could hardly get out of bed. My sister, Lori, who was staying with me while she worked as an intern at *Philadelphia* magazine, had to lift my legs from the mattress to the floor. No sooner was I up than my film editor, Allen Kohler, called to say we would have to re-shoot—the film didn't come out. It was a couple of weeks before my muscles relaxed enough for me to rerun the course, and ultimately I had to run it a third time for new camera angles. The film was almost two years in the making because it took the Justice Department that long to reach their decision—that some women could handle the work, some couldn't, and those who wanted to try should be granted the opportunity. By federal court ruling, city detective work was at last opened up to women. Today 17 of Philadelphia's 572 detectives are women, 2 of them sergeants, the highest rank yet attained in the city.

While covering the police beat as a general assignment reporter, I met a young female D.A. who was involved in Philadelphia's rape crisis center, the first of its kind in the country. Rape was the nation's most underreported crime, yet no local station had tackled the subject for television. I told my news director I wanted to do the story

"You want to do a story on rape?" he said incredulously. "On the 6:00 news? When people are *eating?*"

"I'm just asking you if I can do a report," I answered. "I don't want to do a live demonstration."

He thought about it for a while and at last agreed, but only to running it on the 11:00 news.

We spread it over five evenings, and thus the five-part series was born. The concept was copied all over the country and is still a popular format on local news shows. There were so many requests from viewers to rerun it—"I thought the documentary on rape was wonderful. The only problem was, my ten-year-old had school the next day. Could you please rerun it at 6:00?"—that we aired it again. Viewed in legislatures in Pennsylvania, New Jersey, and Delaware, the series was partially responsible for changing laws concerning the treatment of rape victims and the prosecution of rapists in all three states.

Months after the series aired, I gave a speech at Beaver College, and afterwards a woman tapped me on the shoulder. "I came here tonight to tell you in person something I have wanted to tell you for a long time," she said. "I watched your show on rape, and a few days later when I was walking home from work I was attacked. But I had bought a whistle because I remembered your saying it was a good way to summon help. I blew it as loud as I could, and that rapist ran like hell. You saved me from getting raped, and you might have saved my life . . . and I just want to thank you." Anytime reporters can see a story they have presented be translated directly into viewer action or become a catalyst for societal change, it is more satisfying than any award that could possibly be won.

Chapter 10

My promotion to co-anchor was not met with jubilant cheers by the two men with whom I would be working, Mort Crim and Vince Leonard. Mort clearly did not need me; he already had a number-one-rated show at 5:30. Vince Leonard had long been dean of anchormen in the Delaware Valley. They took me out to dinner and told me that, of all the things that had happened to them in their lifetimes, this was not one of their favorites. Mort was at that time in his late thirties and Vince in his midforties, and they had already been in the business twenty years or more. I explained that I did not want them to carry my weight, that I would work hard and do my very best. I *did* do my best—with their help—and it turned into two winning combinations. We liked each other personally and respected each other professionally, and I learned a great deal from both of them.

Mort was responsible for persuading me to do public speaking. He was a superb speaker, one of the most popular then in Philadelphia—and now in Detroit, where he is principal anchor for WDIV-TV and substitute anchor for the popular Paul Harvey radio show. It would be possible, he said, for me to earn $300 giving speeches to local groups. That intrigued me, and I accompanied Mort to a speech he gave to the local Junior Chamber of Commerce, during which I decided I would never be able to deliver three dollars worth, let alone three *hundred* dollars worth, in person. Although I was entirely relaxed on camera, if I had to stand up and say something to an assembled group of people whom I could actually see, I was rendered all but inarticulate. My hands got clammy, my knees shook, and I reverted to my lisp. Mort insisted it would be necessary for me to overcome this fear if I were to make it in the business beyond the local studio. He promised that if I accepted a speaking engagement, he would go with me.

I agreed to appear before the Frankford Lions Club, and when a member, Whitman Rice, picked me up, I couldn't conceal my terror. "You know," he soothed, "it doesn't really matter what you say.

They just want to see their local newscaster in person." He must have been right, because it seemed to go all right.

I was next contracted by Rita Rappaport, owner of the Blum Store chain, to speak to the Jeff Fund for Children's Colitis. Rita is responsible for my "packaging," if such a thing exists. I couldn't afford to appear in a new outfit every night, so Rita generously lent me five outfits a week to wear even though we were not allowed to give her credit on air (I promised to tell anyone who asked me off-camera, however). She simplified my look, knowing I had to wear what was most expedient. I couldn't go out on assignment in ruffles and pearls, but on the other hand, I had to spruce up my act for the camera. She chose tailored shirts and slacks for day, which I embellished with a blazer and scarf for my newscast. My job dictated the style, and Rita carried it out.

What lecturing brought me was the opportunity to go into different parts of the community, to meet people from all walks of life. Not only were the speeches a way of augmenting my income, I got, in the bargain, a feel for my audience—what they looked like, what they thought, what they were interested in. Audience questions beyond, "Do you sit on a pillow to make you look taller?" (Yes) or, "Do you put highlights in your hair?" (No, Lesley Blanchard does) often provide or define areas of interest useful in formulating ideas for stories. I continued lecturing even when I got to the network, trying to visit areas of the country outside the Washington–New York–Boston corridor. To cover network news successfully is to truly believe that there is life past the Hudson and before the LA city limits.

One of the most intoxicating moments in my career for my mother—who by now had forgotten all the Sturm und Drang of the past—was the day I delivered a speech to the Chester County, Pennsylvania, Association at Longwood Gardens. My mother accompanied me, and when we pulled into the parking lot, the man who opened the door said, "Well, if it isn't Mrs. Savitch and Jessica." "Oh, my goodness!" my mother exclaimed, clapping her cheek. "The mailman from Taylor Street and he recognized us! Jessica, isn't that wonderful?" It may have taken the mailman to do it, but I had finally impressed my mother. For her, this event was a legitimate career triumph.

———————— • ————————

Vince Leonard was an extraordinarily spirited man who sincerely loved the business. He had an impeccable sense of timing, and more importantly, he had integrity. When you watch someone like Vince work every night, you begin to pick up good habits purely by osmosis: the necessity of caring, of getting involved, of conscientiously checking sources for accuracy. Among the most useful things he taught me was to take reviews with a grain of salt.

One night I came in to do the news, and just before I went on I picked up the paper to check out the TV listings. The entertainment section was missing. I looked through another paper, and then another and finally through every *Bulletin* in the office. "Hey! Who's got all the TV pages?" I called out. Nobody answered. I went into Vince's office and said, "Let me see your newspaper." He handed it to me. No TV page. "What's going on here?" I asked. "Why don't we talk about it when you get off the air?" he said. "Tell me what's on that page," I demanded. And he told me. "An article about you that is not favorable. But I don't think we need to discuss it now." I went on and did the news, and afterwards he brought the review out of hiding. "All through the years," Vince said, "I've gotten lousy reviews, but I never read them until I went off the air. I feel terrible for a while, and then figure the reviewer is an idiot."

Overall I have not had many negative articles. Still, the hateful letter comes in with predictable regularity: "Get off the air. You sound like a frustrated telephone operator." The same is true for telephone tirades. The first night I was on the air in Houston, a man called after the early newscast and shouted, "I think you stink! Who ever said women could do news shows?" He called me back after the 10:00 news to tell me he hated me then, too.

I compare my negative reviews to those of some of my colleagues, and I know I have been fortunate. However, the few that have been written about me I could probably quote verbatim. The good ones that come from top-notch personality reporters like Liz Smith, syndicated by the *Daily News*, or Rona Barrett, who worked with NBC, give me a temporary rush of pride, and then I send them on to my mother. But the bad ones—I memorize every word. Every nasty word. And it hurts. It always hurts.

Television is personal, it is you and the viewer. When you are rejected, it is hard not to take it personally, and in this industry you are constantly open for rejection. It takes a great deal of strength to survive it.

I recall an interview Gene Shalit did with Barbara Walters for *Ladies' Home Journal*, in which she described how ghastly her first few months at ABC were. Harry Reasoner just plain didn't want her on the show, and everybody knew it. Some people at the network wouldn't talk to her. The press lambasted her. The afternoon newspaper would arrive, and before she opened it, she knew she would be taking yet another blast. She was barely able to stop crying in time to go on the air. It was the worst time of her life—despite the million-dollar contract, the *Time* cover, the *good* press. If you are consistently attacked in that way, it is as though you have been rejected by someone in a close relationship.

There are still criticisms that crop up about me, primarily that I have achieved too much too soon, before I was really ready. I don't exactly know what it means to be ready. A cake when the oven timer goes off? That's what I always think of: Am I fully baked, or only half-baked?

Chapter
11

It was in Philadelphia that I became aware of just how crucial ratings are. Until the sixties, local news was merely a write-off, according to an FCC ruling of 1934, "to serve the interest, convenience and necessity of the public." A news reader, usually from the radio side of the station, stood in front of a lectern and recited copy, giving rise to the idea that television people were disembodied heads. There were no sponsors, no visual material, no frills.

Gradually, executives realized that viewers were as interested in what happened in their own communities as what happened on Capitol Hill or around the globe. Locally originated news was added, and then expanded, and then embellished by sports, weather, features, and consumer reports. The result was that the newscast ultimately became an imagemaker, as well as the biggest moneymaker, for the local stations. In a market as large as Philadelphia, one rating point translates into a million dollars worth of sales revenue. This accounts for the widespread panic engendered by the seasonal ratings war.

During one siege, I got intestinal flu—one of those really devastating foreign imports that makes death look like a godsend. I called in to Channel 3 to say I thought I was dying. "You won't be in?!" the program director screamed. "Jessica! It's *ratings!*"

"I know it's ratings. But I have intestinal flu. Bad intestinal flu."

"How bad is bad?"

"Bad enough that I'm spending most of my time in the bathroom."

"But we're in ratings!"

"Bob, I'm sorry. I am throwing up every half hour."

"Tell you what. It's only 11:00 in the morning. Why don't we see how you're doing closer to news time?"

"Fine, Bob. Let's see how I'm doing closer to news time."

Bob called me every hour.

"Hi, sweetie. You OK? Feeling better? When's the last time you threw up?"

This went on until 4:30, one hour before the news. He called again, whimpering, "Jessica. Listen, please. You won't have to write the news, I promise. But we need you. Listen. Here's the deal: Couldn't you come in, and if you have to, you can throw up during the commercial breaks. I put a trash bucket under your desk."

In the end, I gave in and did the 11:00 news.

Whether they were ever able to determine if my not being on the 5:30 newscast cost them share points, I don't know. But that is how critical ratings are at a local station.

———————— • ————————

On another occasion, I was working on a five-part series about natural childbirth—the first ever done for local television. For months I followed a couple all the way through the woman's pregnancy. Ads appeared in *TV Guide* four weeks in advance of air time. A few days before the series was to air, the baby had not yet arrived. We had filmed the first three segments; parts four and five were to focus on the actual birth of the child and the family going home. I went to my news director.

"Mrs. Condello is late."

"But we've already got the *TV Guide* ads," he

said. "We've got to run it. We've got to get those last two parts."

"I know you have the ads, but I don't have the baby."

"We're in ratings, damn it, and we've bought the ads."

"Well, what do you want me to do? Mrs. Condello hasn't delivered."

"I don't know what I want you to do . . . Wait, I've got a terrific idea! Can you get her to induce labor?"

"Induce labor?!? The series is about *natural* childbirth!"

As far as he was concerned, I shouldn't let nature stand in the way of a good story. So I stayed up all night with Joe Vandergast and Paul Dowie, my cameramen, and Allen Kohler, my editor. Their wives, Carol, Doris, and Bernice, came in and helped as well. Together we found out the names of every woman having a baby by natural childbirth who was due in the next forty-eight hours in the Delaware Valley. Even though we wouldn't have the same couple we would at least have a birth and a going-home scene. The following evening we were all having dinner in a Chinese restaurant when we were paged by Mr. Condello. His wife had gone into labor!

The birth of Sarah Margaret Condello was one of the most uplifting experiences of my life, and the series went on to sweep all the local awards for best news feature.

The pressure for ratings has increased in the seven or eight years since those incidents. In top markets such as New York and Los Angeles, local newscasters now get overnight ratings; if they're low, it's a real kick in the teeth. How good you are on the air definitely affects how good you feel about yourself—but how good *can* you feel when you see yourself rated instantly every day? Ratings are not necessarily directly attributable to your ability. Sometimes if NBC has a bad program line-up, or CBS has a show on at 10:00 that you don't want to watch, the 11:00 newscasters will get low ratings because you're still tuned in to ABC.

One reason I left local news was that I was tired of this biannual bloodletting. I was also tired of the constant musical chairs among news directors. I was in Philadelphia a little over four years, and I went through five news directors, which meant that every few months there was somebody new wanting to put his personal stamp on the product.

That kind of turnover inevitably produces friction and tension. I looked at the networks and thought, *there's* stability. Dick Wald had been president of NBC News for years, as had Dick Salant of CBS and Bill Sheehan of ABC. But almost as soon as I arrived, the networks began to emulate the local stations. In the five years I have been at NBC, I have worked for four presidents!

During the last year of my contract in Philadelphia, I anchored the coverage for the Ford–Carter debates at the Walnut Street Theatre. I knew that all the network people would be in town, and I wanted to do really well on the air. I was particularly aware that NBC would keep close watch on KYW, since we were an affiliate. Earlier that evening I met Bob Mulholland, NBC's vice president in charge of specials for news, who was exceedingly cordial. A shiver went down my spine, and I was more than ever excited about him seeing me do my field bit.

I pretaped my opening, working fastidiously on my delivery; unfortunately, the KYW computers rolled the promo a few seconds late. I was still talking when the network went on-air, cutting out the beginning of John Chancellor's opening. Instead of hearing the announcer say, "From the Walnut Street Theatre in Philadelphia, this is an NBC News special presentation. Now here is John Chancellor," all that was picked up was the end of Chancellor's name . . . "or."

Bob Mulholland came tearing out of the remote truck. "What happened? What did you do?" he cried. "You ruined John Chancellor's opening!" All I could say was, "I'm sorry," and all I could think was, "Thank God there are two other net-

works, because I'll never work for NBC." Bob
Mulholland has told everybody about that incident. Later he sent me a tongue-in-cheek memo
saying he would forgive me, but he would never
forget.

When at last my contract with KYW neared its
end in 1977, I entered into negotiations with the
networks. I was fortunate in my timing; all three
were interested in talking to a woman with my experience. The best potential for solid experience,
however, was the offer from Don Meaney, vice
president at NBC's bureau in Washington: a Senate correspondency and anchor position on *Sunday Night News* and on *Update*.

As unhappy as I often was at KYW, I see it in
retrospect as a period of maturation. Had I gone
straight to the network, I would have failed
abysmally. I needed to grow up as a journalist.

Chapter
12

I stayed at Channel 3 until Labor Day weekend 1977, then loaded up my car, drove to Washington, and started at NBC the following Monday. For three months NBC put me up at the Watergate Towers while I searched for a place of my own. Finally I rented an apartment on Massachusetts Avenue, a beautiful duplex near the bureau.

My highly publicized arrival at NBC rankled a lot of people. My NBC advance promotion was exaggerated in many publications, which often fabricated a salary of preposterous heights. Since it is my belief that one's salary is between an individual and the IRS, I declined comment. That proved little deterrent. US magazine photographed me at the bureau even before I officially started. There was also a feeling that I hadn't proved myself in the trenches. The trenches at the network are identified as any one of its own, or another network's, foreign bureaus or domestic bureaus outside New York or Washington. It does no good to recount scoops, scrapes, close calls or award winners in any local market, including the top five. If you didn't do it at the network, it doesn't count. Thus, though I'd worked in broadcasting since age fifteen, I was categorized as a beginner, pigeonholed as a glossy blond news reader hired to dress the set and fill out the minority hiring quotas.

Moreover, there was resentment that I had been chosen over women already at the network. In truth, stations did have a double standard in selecting newscasters. When the FCC demanded evidence that women were being given equal opportunities, many stations simply plucked up the most attractive secretary in the office and put her on the air. Men, on the other hand, had to prove themselves by building up their credentials over a long period of time.

When *CBS Morning News* was looking for a woman to co-anchor with Hughes Rudd, where did they go to find her? Not to local stations, or to seasoned reporters—Lesley Stahl, Catherine Mackin, Connie Chung, Marya McLaughlin, Liz Trotta, Sylvia Chase, Betty Rollins, Judy Woodruff, Linda Ellerbee, Carole Simpson—all of them worthy candidates. They chose Sally Quinn. She was a star *Washington Post* reporter, and certainly a fine print journalist, but she had no television experience whatsoever. And she couldn't handle the job. I don't fault Sally Quinn; I fault those who hired her.

The other women who failed when suddenly thrust on the air were, by the same token, victimized. They weren't given time to learn. I heard one of them refer to the international easing of tension as Dante with Russia, and I wondered what circle of hell *that* was. Another said, "Politicians and people alike are upset by what happened at city hall today." Well, maybe she was on to something there; whether all politicians *are* people does give pause for thought.

In any case, many of these arbitrary promotions meant that a man who had spent years moving up the ranks, from Clearwater, Florida, to Yuma, Arizona and on to his big break in Denver, suddenly found himself teamed with, or passed over for, an ex-Miss Peach Blossom—and he was furious. The rest of the women who had worked their way up were furious, too.

When I arrived at NBC, just about everyone ignored me. Carole Simpson was one of the few exceptions, and I will be unendingly grateful for her kindness those first few weeks. Tensions did ease somewhat after it became clear that I did not breeze out of a limousine each morning, trailed by a hairdresser and makeup man.

Once I actually began working, I found the job itself endlessly fascinating. As Washington correspondent, I covered the Senate, and my first assignment was to report on the Humphrey–Hawkins unemployment bill. I knew no one in the Senate, nor did I know anyone who *did* know anyone. The Washington bureau chief had just left, and Sid Davis, who was to take his place, had not yet taken over. All the old Texas anxieties came racing back, full throttle.

I made what seemed like an endless series of phone calls to government officials such as press reps in the Humphrey–Hawkins offices and higher-ups in the Bureau of Labor Statistics, to get as much of a grounding on the issue as I could, then headed on over to the Capitol.

A guard pointed the way to the press gallery, where I found a chair and made myself at home. I was beginning to feel more comfortable. So far so good. With my notebook and freshly sharpened pencils in hand, I went to look out over the Senate floor to scan the action, and back up to the gallery to wait for a possible call from the NBC desk. No one came. Later that morning I ran into Marya McLaughlin at a senate hearing. "C'mon," she said, "I'll walk you back to the gallery." Which she did. Only it was not the gallery in which I had been sitting. Marya went to the television-radio gallery. I had been wasting my time in the print gallery.

The Bert Lance scandal broke that week, and Gordon Manning, head of Special Projects at NBC, called to say he wanted a story on reaction to the news. I ran around buttonholing senators and wrote a piece for the 11:30 special report. No field producer was there to assist me. I didn't even know I was supposed to ask for one. I didn't, in fact, know enough to ask *any* of the right questions. All I was told that day was that the crew would be waiting for me at "Elsight." At least that's what I wrote in my notebook. I got myself together and rigged up my tape recorder so I could play my story back through the earphones hidden beneath my hair. Then I went outside and asked a police officer where Elsight Street was. "Sorry, lady, never heard of it," he said. I asked a passerby. "Elsight," he repeated. "Elsight. Hmmmm. I think maybe it's around the back of the building. By now it was nearly dark and I was close to tears. Finally I ran back to the press gallery and called the NBC desk.

"Listen, it's Savitch . . ."

"Where *are* you?"

"I'm out looking for the crew. There's no such place as Elsight Street."

"What? It's Elmsite. *Elm*site. Look out front."

Sure enough, I saw the lights across the way, under a big tree. Elmsite, so named for the large elm in front of the Capitol, is the familiar back-drop for Washington correspondents.

Capitol Hill stand-ups are customarily shot out-side so that the cameraman can take advantage of the natural light. Even when the driving snow plasters your hair to your face, you brave it in the outdoors. I have often wondered how viewers could believe anything said by a woman too stupid to come in from a blizzard, but producers are ap-parently convinced that a view of the elm or the iron horse or the Capitol dome gives the story depth. In late afternoon, Elmsite gets dark rapidly because the tree throws a dense shade. On the other hand, the iron horse at the back of the Cap-itol is perched on one of the windiest spots in Washington. Still correspondents are always told to get the best shot of the Capitol dome. We went through a stage at NBC during which it was essen-tial to capture the whole dome on film. To do so, cameramen had to get down on their hands and knees and shoot upwards from tripods only inches high—an angle even more unflattering than it is improbable, freakishly elongating the newscaster like an Aubrey Beardsley figure.

———— • ————

My second major assignment was to trail Vice President Mondale through the West and Northwest. The Carter administration had never been very popular in that area, and this whirlwind jaunt was a way of mending fences. After skimming twelve states in four days, I returned to Washington about 1 A.M. and fell into my bed in a dull exhaustion. Early the next morning I got a call from the desk editor, Susan LaSalla, telling me that Hubert Humphrey had just died, and I was to cover the funeral.

I stood next to the catafalque in the rotunda, and I remembered the immense impression Kennedy's funeral had made on me when I watched it on television. In real life, events seem much less dramatic. Television is an eye that sees selectively, ignoring the mourners chewing gum and officials organizing themselves for the processional.

For the most part, covering the Senate was a routine affair but I was busy the first few months learning the Senate rules, not to mention when and where newscasters and cameras were allowed. Cameras are forbidden, for instance, in the Senate chambers, so senators are called off the floor to be interviewed in the gallery, a tiny, two-story alcove just across from the visitors' gallery. A choice of three backdrops is used—a burnished gold curtain, an icy blue wall, and what looks like a set of law volumes. Many senators have developed a canny sense of what will play best for the audience. "I think what I'm wearing today would look better against the blue," or "CBS interviewed me just a minute ago in front of the books—maybe we ought to try the curtain this time."

———————— • ————————

The most important event I covered was the Panama Canal debate, which dragged on for months. At the end of the session, key bills had piled up and millions of dollars worth of appropriations for government programs were voted on in the last forty-eight hours of the Ninety-fifth Congress. It leads one to suspect that unworkable programs are in many cases funded because legislators are just too tired to make reasonable decisions. I remember seeing one befuddled senator come out on the Senate floor and ask, "Is this one up or down? What is it we're voting on anyway?"

In advance of the Panama Canal debate, I traveled with the Senate Foreign Relations Committee, as well as other key senators, on a junket to Panama headed by then Senate Majority Leader Robert Byrd. General Omar Torrijos led us on a tour of the Canal Zone, which included an excursion by boat to an outer island.

Afterwards, I pooled resources with the correspondents from ABC and CBS to charter a plane back to the mainland. Our field producers, who had taken our morning footage with them to edit in the hotel, were to meet the plane, race us back to write, edit, and feed the second half of our stories to the networks for the 6:30 newscast. The ABC producer was waiting when we arrived, as was the CBS producer. Jim Lee, my producer, was nowhere in sight. I waited for thirty minutes and then grabbed a taxi to the hotel. I knocked on the door of the room in which Jim and the tape editor, Nelson Martinez, were supposed to be editing, but no one answered.

"*Dónde está* Sr. Lee and Sr. Martinez?" I asked the desk clerk.

"Ah, ah, ah, *señorita*. Ahh, *están en la carcel.*"

"Jail?"

"*Sí, sí.*"

As it happened, Nelson Martinez had gotten into an argument with a border guard who insisted on opening all the luggage. He was instantly marked as a troublemaker. The police visited his hotel room, accusing him of having marijuana. Then they proceeded to pull a joint out of a shoe. He and Jim Lee had never seen the grass before.

Frantically, I placed a call to Don Meaney in Washington, who in turn called Richard Valeriani, the State Department correspondent, and within a couple of hours Jim and Nelson were released. They got back just in time to get our feed together for the satellite. Thus, I became the only correspondent at NBC to have a good war story without having to go to a war zone.

My transition out of the Senate correspondency

was made after the off-year elections of 1978, my most critical assignment to that point. It was my misfortune, however, to have the assignment coincide with some minor but necessary surgery. Had I been a good patient, I would have been laid up for several weeks.

Ten days after my operation, I went back on air. I had not wanted NBC to know the extent of my sickness since I might lose the opportunity that meant so much to me.

Although my health remained shaky, I did cover the Senate race. Tom Brokaw reported the House and gubernatorial campaigns and John Chancellor and David Brinkley the overall election returns. I was aware from the outset that I was the weakest link in the chain. I went to the Senate and interviewed every incumbent running for re-election, did phone interviews with their opponents, and flew to several states to follow key races, including the Hathaway–Cohen race in Maine. I trudged around with Hathaway all day and on to a bean supper at the East Sangerville, Maine, Grange—a political farm organization. The first thing Susan LaSalla and I asked for was the rest room. The code of the road is, if there is anything to eat, eat; if there is a place to sit, sit; if there is a restroom, go. You might not find another for hours. This time our question was answered with a gruff, "Out there." And "out there" was literal. I wondered, as I sat freezing my posterior in the outhouse, how anyone ever got the notion my job was glamorous.

On 3″ × 5″ index cards, I recorded every useful bit of information and every colorful anecdote I had gathered in my election night preparation. With the help of Roberta Spring, production associate of *Nightly News,* and my former assistant, Carol Levine, I typed and then filed them in a little green index card box my nephews David and Michael donated for good luck. Although I knew I was fully prepared, I was still terrified.

Before air time Tom Brokaw came to my dressing room and said, "There is not one person out there who doesn't think you can do the job." When it was all over, Tom, as well as John David and Executive Producer Les Crystal, said it had gone splendidly. The ratings later confirmed their assessment. Obviously, all those months of being cooped up in the Senate gallery served me well. I only used about one-tenth of the anecdotal material I had collected, but the rest came in handy at cocktail parties for the next three years.

Chapter
13

After two years as a Senate correspondent, I was appointed to do the NBC magazine show, *Prime Time Sunday*, with Tom Snyder. Tom preceded me in Philadelphia at WRCV-TV, which later became KYW. Even then he was a colorful, controversial figure. He was highly respected by those who worked closely with him, particularly cameramen—who see correspondents at their best and worst. I was told that Tom would go out to do a story on, say, a public school, and he would tell the cameraman: "Look, get about eight seconds of those kids over there, and give me five seconds on a swing shot, then a long shoot zooming into the school." While the shots were being executed, he did his stand-up, and the crew couldn't make heads or tails of what he was trying to achieve. But he would go back to the studio, piece the whole thing together, and produce a terrific story.

Outrageousness was his trademark. Not long after he joined the station, he created the James Tate Award. Each week he would give it to the person or organization who had committed what Tom considered the most egregious act of the week.

James Tate was the mayor of Philadelphia, and this award so infuriated him that he called the management and demanded Tom's insults cease at once. The winner of the James Tate Award that week was James Tate.

Occasionally I filled in on the *Tomorrow Show,* an experience that gave me a greater appreciation of Tom's talents. There was just a chair and a city scene backdrop—no script, no news event, no co-host with whom you could ad lib. Tom is a past master at the intimate one-to-one conversation, a natural talent who makes television viewers feel he is talking directly to them.

What I found compelling about the *Tomorrow Show* was the unstructured format, one perfectly suited to Tom's easygoing, personable style. *NBC Magazine,* although still in its formulative stages, was a good show but whether it was good for Tom Snyder is another question.

I was lucky enough to do several pieces I thought significant on the stockpiling of nerve gas by the Soviets, cancer and THC, vasectomy reconnection, and even one called "The Logo Gypsy," about local anchor people. The name of the game in the industry is to gypsy around the country, starting, say, in the twentieth largest market, with a promotion logo of "Action News," to a number nine market with an "Eyewitness News" logo in a year or two, then onward and upward.

The first feature I did was with producer Susan Ludel on Jane Fonda and Tom Hayden, who were traveling coast to coast on behalf of their Campaign for Economic Democracy. I flew out to Malibu to interview them in their modest bungalow, and while the lights were being set up I had the chance to talk to Jane about *The China Syndrome,* in which she played a reporter who covered the fluff beat for a local television station. She battles to do more significant pieces, and, because she is articulate, involved and intelligent, you really believe she can. When she is finally assigned to cover a potential meltdown at a nuclear plant, she uses her ingenuity to track sources and film under cover. When she finally reports the story, she bursts into tears, rendering her all but inarticulate, incapable of doing her job of communicating the story to the public. I mentioned to her that an actual TV newscaster probably would not cry, but

Jane defended the movie's position, saying the ending made "better theater."

How valuable *NBC Magazine* was in my career is questionable. A series of executive producers and on-air talent came and went, and the time slot was shifted several times. Notwithstanding the fine moments, this was among the more frustrating assignments.

Chapter
14

Although I knew that ultimately my answerability was to the viewer, I very much wanted to be accepted by my peers, to be considered a serious journalist. I earned a small measure of respect when I anchored an unscripted report of the killings of Congressman Leo Ryan, correspondent Don Harris, and cameraman Bob Brown on the airstrip in Guyana. All anyone knew at NBC was that two of our own had been shot down in Guyana.

I was called late Saturday night and given sketchy details—word had not reached us of the mass suicide. Instead of leaving for New York Sunday morning on the 10:00 shuttle, I took the earliest possible milk train. All day we waited in vain for footage to arrive; finally, NBC, at the direction of the News Vice President Ed Planer, decided to charter a Learjet and send news executive Don Dunkle to Guyana to pick up field producer Bob Flick with footage and fly on to Puerto Rico, the nearest satellite point. Flick would then go into the studio and let me get a voice-track report for the newscast. Two minutes into our interviews, it became clear to me that Flick was not yet up to looking at footage showing his friends' death. I went back to the nightly newsroom at 6:20. Producer Bill Chesleigh, who had supervised the feed from Puerto Rico, told Herb Dudnick, "Flick is in no shape to script and narrate the lead spot." It was now eight minutes to air. "Then who's going to do the story?" I asked Herb. Dead silence. Herb stared at me. Chesleigh stared at me. I got the message. We had no report, only raw footage we had not even had time to screen. I would view it for the first time on the air, with the rest of the audience, and narrate what I saw, or at least try.

Along with millions of viewers, I saw my colleague Don Harris throwing away his cigarette in preparation for boarding the aircraft. Then the cult members, pulling up on a flatbed truck and blasting away at Congressman Leo Ryan, Don Harris and others. NBC cameraman Bob Brown, topnotch newsman that he was, kept shooting. So did the cult members. Brown shot tape. They reeled off live ammunition. Brown went down rolling, and the tape faded to black as Brown's own life faded away. There was shocked, grieved silence in the control room, and before I could stop myself I said "Unbelievable . . ."—a word a staff member later had printed in large letters and framed for my office. News people are trained to run toward danger, not from it, and Bob Brown's heroism affected me deeply.

After that newscast, I won over Herb Dudnick, then executive producer of *NBC Weekend Nightly News* (he now holds that position on NBC's new late night newscast), whose attitude, I imagine, had been much like that of the rest of the staff: "So she reads well. But can she report?" Gaining his respect was a boon to my career, because he was an excellent teacher.

———————— • ————————

The real breakthrough came three years after my arrival. Les Crystal, executive producer of the presidential elections, called to tell me I would be podium correspondent at both of the national conventions and anchor the House and gubernatorial desk on election night. As I had done during the off-year elections, I began my arduous preparations.

Drew Lewis, now Secretary of Transportation,

and his associate Rick Robb, coached me in campaign routine. Ensconcing myself in the videotape library at Vanderbilt University in Nashville, I viewed tapes of the 1976 conventions to observe the performances of the anchors from all three networks. I visited eight states in which Democrats had initiated Dump Carter or Draft Kennedy committees. Trailing candidates dictated a schedule so punishing that one night I fell asleep in my hotel at 4 A.M. fully clothed and woke a couple of hours later, not knowing where I was. I picked up the phone and wondered how I was going to get the operator to tell me where I was without actually asking her the name of the town. I decided to inquire about the morning paper, hoping it would have an identifying name.

"Good morning, Miss Savitch."

"Uh, yes. Good morning. Do you have a paper?"

"Sorry, not this early."

"How about a phone book?"

"If you'd just tell me who you'd like, I'd be glad to get the number for you."

I began to panic. "Er, no, that's OK. Never mind. I think I'll go out for breakfast."

"Fine. Oh, Miss Savitch?"

"Yes?"

"Welcome to Omaha."

"Thank you!" I blurted. "You don't know how good it is to know I'm in Omaha!"

I looked forward to the one-on-one competition with other network newscasters, but I was also scared. Two strikes were already against me. I was in contract negotiations, having fulfilled my original three year stint; to fail would mean the end of the road. And I was to be podium correspondent, which would put me at a disadvantage. I would not have access to first-hand information or breaking stories on the floor.

In order not to be scooped, I knew I had to lay the proper groundwork. Washington bureau chief Sid Davis, a thorough, hard-working man who was producing the podium coverage for the first time, advised me: "Knock on doors, dial that phone, pound the corridors; wear out the old shoe leather." He was an invaluable aid and inspiration.

I found out who the parliamentarians were, introduced myself and told them, "Please remember me—I'll be sitting over there, and I'll need all the information you can give me." I went around to all the key people, including the guards, and flat out confessed: "I'm going into my first convention and I need your help. I promise you a fair job in return." That is the closest I ever came to begging. But the elections are the Olympics of newscasting: If you blow it, you have a four-year wait before you can try again, if indeed you are given the chance to try again.

Each network was allowed two seats—one for a reporter and one for a producer—on the podium.

I had anchored the entire podium coverage so far, but as the clock ticked closer to the final address by President Carter, the networks began their shuffle games. ABC's producer left and correspondent Sam Donaldson, their heavy hitter, was sent up to sit with Jimmy Wooten. CBS replaced their producer and anchor Bruce Morton with Lesley Stahl and Ed Bradley. Then Sid David was called off by NBC and Tom Pettit joined me. So there were now six network correspondents sitting on the podium, until the rules committee delivered the ultimatum: Two correspondents could sit on the podium, but only one could wear a headset and report. Jimmy Wooten took off his headset. Ed Bradley took off his. And, to my dismay, I was ordered by my producer to take off mine. Tom Pettit would replace me as podium correspondent. One does not argue in tight, competitive field situations. Pettit was, after all, the senior correspondent. Logic like that didn't help. I was devastated.

As soon as President Carter finished his speech, there was a free-for-all. I could see that he was making moves to leave, so I clapped on my headset and shoved my way to the other side of the room. I looked over at Tom Pettit surrounded by the reporters from the other networks trying to block the veteran convention correspondent. Pettit gave me thumbs up. Engineer Carmine Picioccio rolled out the extra cable he'd kept hidden to enable me to climb the barrier between the president and the press. "Please let me through the barrier," I pleaded with a guard I had gotten to know. "Now, you know I can't let you through, Jessica," he said and paused. "But I can't help it if I don't see you sneak past me, can I?"

In the crush I got around to the president as he left the stage. I was, in fact, the only correspondent from any of the three networks who did get to him. It was not exactly an earthshaking interview: I simply asked him a couple of questions about Kennedy and party unity. Everybody saw it, but by the time the other reporters rushed over, we were already being knocked to the floor by the Secret Service. The president had gone. Tom Pettit, who had done a superb job, joked to me later, "Next time, Savitch, *you* block and *I'll* carry the ball."

The Republican convention was one of the most thrilling events of my career. It was widely rumored that Gerald Ford was to be Ronald Reagan's running mate. All the network newscasters— Walter Cronkite, Dan Rather, Frank Reynolds— everybody was reporting it more or less as a *fait accompli*. I had three monitors on the podium, and I could hear Walter discussing how a co-presidency would work; I could hear Ted Koppel and Frank Reynolds talking about how the deal had been negotiated. NBC at this point was lagging behind in the coverage.

Sid Davis spotted Senator Paul Laxalt, known

Reagan confidant and a good source. Sid cornered him, and when I questioned him on the air, Laxalt revealed that he knew for a certainty that everyone was on the wrong track. Ford was *not* going to be Reagan's choice. Exactly who was, according to Laxalt, was at that moment being decided. A few minutes later, NBC correspondent Chris Wallace cornered a key delegate who said Reagan's choice would be George Bush. NBC now not only beat the competition but also came from behind to lead the coverage.

Although the average viewer is not going to remember these details, they did make life easier for me at NBC. Those who felt that I had had things handed to me on a silver platter began to accept the fact that I was willing to go out there and hustle with the rest of them. For the first time, I felt like part of the news team.

———— • ————

I had expected that when I finally got to the network I would hear a hallelujah chorus in the background. I once read a poem about a woman who climbs a mountain to see the view. At the end of the day she realizes she must have passed the top, because the rest of the way was downhill. I too thought I must have somehow by-passed the peak.

The rush of glory actually came four months later. President Sadat was on his way to Jerusalem to negotiate the peace initiative, and NBC expanded the Sunday night news to an hour to present special coverage. I fully anticipated that I would not anchor my newscast that night, and would not have objected even though my contract guaranteed me the right to appear. I was new, and I did not have the experience in foreign affairs that John Chancellor and David Brinkley had.

I could hardly believe my eyes when I went to the assignment bulletins and read that John Chancellor would anchor from Jerusalem, David Brinkley from Washington, and Jessica Savitch from New York.

When I got back to my office, Joe Angotti, executive producer of the nightly news, was on the phone. "I'd like to go over some plans with you for Sunday," Joe said. "I think maybe I'll have you do a pretaped profile on Sadat and Begin, and all other news. How does that sound?" What it sounded like was a dream come true. Instead of figuring "that stupid little girl doesn't know anything about the Mideast; all she knows are street fires in Philadelphia," he took the time to think of something I *could* do.

When the moment came and I was sitting on the set waiting to go on the air, I looked at the monitor and saw John coolly standing in Jerusalem and David coolly smoking a cigarette and shuffling through his papers in Washington and me in New York attempting to look cool. I was overcome. These men were the giants of the industry. Even if I had only read, "Good evening, heavy rainstorms deluged the West Coast, good night," I would have been happy.

———————— • ————————

Anchoring the news is essentially the same in every market, big or small. You're at a desk, you've got a script, you face two cameras and a TelePrompTer, and you do the news. The Sunday I anchored my first network news show was just like any other time—right down to the fumbles.

NBC had decided to change to open sets, meaning that on a wide shot you were seen head to toe. For several days I debated whether or not to wear slacks so I wouldn't have to worry that, while reading the news, I might inadvertently move my legs to an embarrassingly revealing position. My mother insisted slacks were too casual and in the end I decided she was probably right. To protect myself in case I forgot and crossed my legs, I took a piece of thick masking tape—the kind reporters say mends everything but broken hearts—and taped my ankles together. It worked exceedingly well, holding my legs neatly together every time I inadvertently tried to move them. The first open show went without a hitch. When I finished, pleased with my performance, I stood up to shake hands with the crew. I had completely forgotten the tape and tumbled flat on the floor. Luckily the monitors were off, so the entire country did not get to see me literally fall on my face.

Nor did anyone in the audience know that the TelePrompTer jammed as soon as I said "Good evening." Fortunately I was prepared for the emergency, having learned my lesson the hard way while still in Philadelphia. The first time it happened, I hadn't taken a typed script with me, and I watched in horror as the words disappeared in front of me. I had no other copy of the script and no co-anchor to help out. "I'm Jessica Savitch," I said as slowly as I could to give the technician time to unscramble the tape. "This is KYW-TV, Channel 3, Eyewitness News . . ." Nothing was happening. I saw a blur of hands indicating that the TelePrompTer could not be fixed. "We'll have the news, sports and weather coming up right after this message," I said and I waited, dumbly staring at the camera. On-air a second can seem like a year. Finally we cut to a commercial, at which point I bounded back to the news room and grabbed a copy of the script. From then on, I never relied solely on the TelePrompTer.

As far back as Texas, I discovered that weekend anchors must be trained for emergencies. Crews are either still in training or comprised of old-timers who are just filling out their days waiting to retire.

In Philadelphia I once worked with a novice director and a producer old enough to have lapses of memory. It was a great combo. Whenever they hit a problem, they would scream and argue, and, as a last resort, put me on camera while they settled their differences. My only recourse was to introduce a story, dive under the desk, and wait till the floor manager gave me a "five seconds to air" cue. Then I'd quickly scramble into place and start in again.

On the other hand, mistakes are not always the result of someone's ineptitude. A story can break too late for the editor to polish his script or turn the tape in on time. When you consider that you're putting together a half hour show *live* with news coming in from all over the world, it is a miracle that so many news shows are produced without incident. One evening I came to the last story, a taped piece which was to run three minutes and forty seconds, and I said, "And now this story from California . . ." I paused, waiting for the crew to cut to Los Angeles. Nothing happened. All I saw on the monitor was my increasingly worried face.

Finally the director cut to black. I picked up the phone and said, "What are we going to *do?*"

"Ad lib," said the producer.

"I'm alone. There's no one to ad lib with."

The producer answered by putting me back on the air.

"Well, you've probably figured out by now that we don't have that spot ready," I announced. "So what I think I'll do for those of you who might have missed the first part of this news broadcast . . ." and I turned the script over and just re-read the news until it was time to sign off.

———————— • ————————

In the beginning, I couldn't bear a mistake. I was angry with whoever caused it, and angrier still that I didn't handle it better. Sometimes, the error was so embarrassing that afterwards all I could do was weep. I remember one particularly devastating incident in Philadelphia. I had been working on a documentary and didn't get back to the station until almost 5:20, ten minutes before air time. I was to interview Malcolm Poindexter, a political reporter who had covered a demonstration staged at city hall over economic problems, and then do a cross-talk with consumer reporter Orien Reid.

"I've posted some questions for you on the prompter," my producer told me as I hurried past him to the studio. "Don't worry; everything will be just fine."

The first question came up and I asked Malcolm, "Why have toilet paper prices gone up?" He looked at me as though I'd lost my mind, cleared his throat and gamely tried to answer. "Ahhh, the fluctuation in the price of all items has a bearing on the economy, which . . . ahh . . . which was the issue at city hall today." Unfortunately, I had been skimming my script, not really listening. I looked up and asked, "How about the price of eggs?"

Despite his polite formality, Malcolm appeared to want to strangle me. It was only when Orien Reid came on and I asked about the demonstration that I realized my mistake. Later, I asked the producer if I had really asked Malcolm questions about toilet paper and eggs.

"Yes," he said brightly, "you did. The prompter pages were out of order."

"Oh, no," I moaned, "tell me it's just a bad dream."

I asked newsroom secretary Dianne Garner about what I expected to be a flood of viewer calls.

Amazingly, no one called in.

———— • ————

Probably the worst Sunday night newscast at NBC that ever bore my name was one I didn't do.

————

An anchorwoman from the West Coast named Kelly Lange had signed a contract with an NBC affiliate in Los Angeles, KNBC, giving her three appearances per year on a weekend nightly news show. I was filling in for David Brinkley in Washington, and Kelly Lange was called to fill in for me. Correspondent Phillip Till had taped a story on Bedouin sheep for the newscast, but every time Kelly would introduce the story something else would come up on the monitor—or nothing would come up at all. Finally, she paused and said, "I'm not sure, but here, I think, is Phillip Till." Up came a Bedouin sheep going "baaa, baaaa." At that point, the tape went black. When it came back to Kelly, she said, "I guess this is one of those nights when nothing goes right. Have a good evening. You deserve it."

Since a sizable portion of the viewers subscribe to the all-blondes-on-TV-look-alike theory, the mail on the incident was addressed to me. I received about two hundred letters following that program. Some read, "Congratulations on handling a tough situation in a professional manner," others said, "That was the worst piece of broadcasting I have ever seen." Stifling the urge to thank the former and tell the latter group to write to Kelly, I forwarded both, along with my sincere condolences, my appreciation for the fact that there, but for the grace of God, went I. She showed extraordinary poise under an awful lot of pressure.

Chapter
15

News events are like Texas weather. If you don't like it, wait a minute. So, no working day can be described as typical; indeed, the only constant in the industry is change. I might travel coast to coast to do an interview, as I did when working on a special about El Salvadoran refugees in Los Angeles, then turn right around and fly back in time to do *Update* that night. Even on an ordinary day, when my major task is to answer my mail, the pace is relatively hectic.

Still nothing I have ever done on-air in either radio or television has been tougher than *Update*. Purportedly, the mini-newscast concept was the brainstorm of Bob Mulholland and Los Angeles superagent Ed Hookstratten, who handles Tom

Snyder and Tom Brokaw, among others. Prior to the *Tomorrow Show,* Tom was being readied for a stint on network news, so Bob and Ed devised the one-minute news capsule to introduce him to the nationwide audience. Ideal Toys was offered the package and bought it immediately. It became a huge moneymaker, with a nearly one hundred percent profit. More people see it than any news program NBC does, because it offers them a quick rundown of all the important stories that happened in the last twenty-four hours.

What makes *Update* so difficult is that it is live. If it were taped even an hour earlier, the news could change. We try to cover four or five stories in the one-minute slot—which, in actuality, is only forty-two seconds of copy.

If the tape doesn't roll in a regular newscast, you can always say, "I'm sorry that report is not ready; we'll try to have it for you later in the broadcast." On *Update,* there is no later. Even a word garble will waste up to four or five seconds. Then you really have to speed up, since Richard Berman, talented weekend news editor, and his *Update* counterpart Richard Watt have copy and visuals timed to the split second.

When I first began *Update* in Washington there was a studio maintenance man who seemed as well programmed to my forty-two seconds as I was. Invariably, two minutes before I went on air, he switched on his roaring industrial vacuum cleaner just outside the door. When the studio light went on, it was as if it were some kind of mysterious signal to start cleaning. To the audience the noise was probably no more than the buzz of a bee, but to me it sounded like a B-52. After a few futile attempts to communicate with the man, who apparently spoke no English, the floor manager would walk out and kick the vacuum plug right after saying "thirty seconds." Before the maintenance man could amble back over and put the plug back in, I had finished *Update*.

Split-second judgment on newscasts is crucial. Once in the summer of 1981, a call came in to the news desk at about 9:45 P.M. that Marion Barry, mayor of the District of Columbia, had been shot and was on his way to the hospital. A couple of radio stations had already reported the story but there was nothing on the wires; all we had at this point was rumor. Washington *Update* producer Herb Brubaker went ahead and ordered three slides—"Barry Shot," "Barry Wounded," and "Barry Dead"—and kept trying to find another corroborative source. By air time, we still had no confirmation and my producer and I decided not to use the item. Forty minutes later, the shooting was disclaimed by police reports. It seemed that Mayor Barry was at a friend's house watching television when a bulletin came on informing him that he had been shot and possibly killed. He called that particular station to let them know that reports of his death had been greatly exaggerated.

To get it first is important—but more important is to get it right.

———— • ————

Television news can be an exceedingly frustrating business. On a half hour newscast, less than twenty-two minutes is allotted to the news itself, so a lot of good stories get thrown out. I have often sweated over a story until it was just right, only to have it scrapped because the news changed in the fifteen minutes before air time.

Nearly every reporter I know has been baffled by management's conviction that a wire story is somehow more reliable than a reporter's own eyes and ears. While covering a flood in Texas, I interviewed the civil defense, the area rescue squad, and several survivors by phone. I told the desk editor that the clean-up had begun.

"Are you sure?" he asked.

"Of course I'm sure."

"How do you know?"

"I've talked to people on the scene, and people who have returned from the scene, and they all tell me the same thing."

He paused for a few seconds, pursing his lips

and rubbing his forehead.

"No," he said. "It can't be. AP and UPI say the flooding is still going on."

"In that case," I said, "I think the wire machines are in need of my services!"

Tom Pettit, former Senate correspondent and now executive vice president of NBC News, tells audiences at speeches of a similar experience as a young reporter in the South. He was covering the civil rights movement and got a call from one of the networks in New York about a demonstration that was taking place practically outside Tom's window. Excited at this opportunity to do a report for a major station, Tom quickly offered to do the story.

"Okay, son," the network executive said. "Tell me which of the wire services you have at your offices."

"Well, none, sir. We're just a small station."

"How about feeds from any of the independents?"

"No, sir."

"Well are you following the *New York Times?*"

"I'm afraid not, sir."

"Then how the hell do you know what's going on?"

———————— • ————————

For every two minutes of glamour, there are eight hours of hard work. My only truly heady moment occurred in my second year at NBC when I was called to New York to fill in for John Chancellor on the nightly news. The first taping went without a hitch, which meant that I could make the 8:00 shuttle back to Washington. A car and driver were to be provided to take me back to LaGuardia. I went out the front doors of Rockefeller Plaza and looked around for the usual sedate black car. But apparently none was available on short notice. Instead I saw a pearl gray stretch Mercedes. Inside was a bar, a telephone, and a television. A television! I realized my taped newscast was still on, and I could watch the rest of the show. I turned the set on, settled back in the luxuriant splendor of the limousine, and watched myself anchor a prime time newscast with David Brinkley.

But every time I am in danger of believing the glamour of my own press, some incident inevitably brings me back to earth.

Shopping in a neighborhood supermarket in Washington, I was stopped by a man who said, "Aren't you on television? Wait. Don't tell me, I know who you are. You're Carole Simpson." Carole, on the other hand, told me she was once recognized as one of the Pointer Sisters.

Walking my dog Chewy one morning in New

York I passed two women who were staring at me and overheard one whisper to the other, "You know, if that woman would fix herself up she'd look a lot like Jessica Savitch."

Waiting in the dressing room before an appearance on the *David Letterman Show*, I decided to pass the time looking at the program format. The first segment read, "Jessica Savitch interview." The second, "Jessica Savitch Interview, Cont'd," and the third, "Jessica Savitch Interview Cont'd, or Bob the Dog." What that meant was that if I bombed, I would get the vaudevillian hook and be replaced by a more entertaining guest—David's dog.

I have even been an unknown celebrity at NBC, stopped at the door by security guards who, even after I give my name, insist on seeing an ID card.

A year after I started working at NBC, the press department had yet to schedule a promotional photography session. In advance of election night publicity, they hastily reeled off some photos at a rehearsal. The picture of me—in rumpled blouse and sans makeup—should have been enough to dispel the theory that I'd gotten the job on my looks. Two years later, the public relations division had a rubber stamp made to imprint the back of my press photos, all of which subsequently identified me as someone called "Jessica *Savage*, NBC News." Later that year I was honored to be the only female presenter on the Dupont-Columbia Awards show. Superimposed on the screen for the audience of millions to see was, in dreadful déjà vu, the name of that other woman, "Jessica *Savage*, NBC News."

Chapter
16

Sometimes I wonder whether it is possible for the television industry to balance public good with private gain. As Eric Sevareid noted in a recent interview with *National Journal*, "A few years ago the news department began to show a profit, and I was worried. I knew it would be looked at differently by top executives when it began to mean millions of dollars for three or four ratings points."

News is a commodity. By now, viewers know they will hear the major news events of the day no matter what station they tune in, so they watch a particular newscaster for one or two reasons: because the channel is already on or because they have an allegiance to a newscaster. Anchors have become as newsworthy as the stories and personalities they cover.

Television, as the nation's top advertising vehicle, is big business. The competition, hype, and political maneuvering are clear indications that news organizations resemble most other industries. Super agents like Richard Leibner negotiate multimillion dollar contracts while stations bid to seduce newscasters from other stations. About the same time Tom Brokaw joined Roger Mudd on *NBC Nightly News* in a publicity blitz, Dan Rather over at CBS took to wearing a sweater every night because its first appearance correlated with a surge in ratings, and ABC rushed to remind the public through full page promotionals in the *New York Times* that it was still number one.

For a while attention was focused on sets. I have seen desks so futuristically styled that anchors could have gotten whiplash turning from camera to camera. During the elections I broadcasted the vote tallies from a freshly redesigned studio. I sat down and began looking for the monitor. Finally I spotted it suspended from the ceiling. Waving over the producer, I suggested that it might seem as though I were expecting Divine Intervention to guide me through the vote talleys. He agreed and went off presumably to attend to it only to return a few minutes later saying that the monitor could not be moved to eye level. The scenic designer had yelped that it would destroy the aesthetics of his work.

The revamping of sets to bolster ratings was referred to by Ron Kershaw as "the rotten blueberry pie approach." A particular brand of pie is not moving off the grocery shelves because customers know it tastes rotten. So the marketing man figures the way to sell it is to put it in a new package. The All New, Greatly Improved, Electric Blue Box appears, and customers buy it only to find out they've been had: Inside is the same old rotten-tasting blueberry pie.

An All New, Greatly Improved set cannot, alone, send ratings soaring. Viewers are too sophisticated now to be fooled by form; they want substance. It's like buying a ticket to see the talking dog. If the dog has nothing to say, no one will go back in the tent a second time. Viewers viscerally know when they're being cheated.

In local markets, news teams seem bent on competing to win the cute chit-chat contest. We in the industry call this Happy Talk News—the ultimate bastardization of a logical journalistic concept originally known as Involvement News. The idea was to create a more conversational framework. Instead of a pontifical, "And now, for sports news with Joe Jones . . . ," it seemed better for the newscaster to lighten things up a bit, saying, "There was a lot of action in Madison Square Garden today. Tell us about it, Joe." But newscasters across the country missed the point. They juxtaposed silly jokes with serious news of union strikes and subway murders, some of them stopping just short of stand-up comedy routines. And it didn't involve viewers, it turned them off.

Some news managers have been slow to grasp that, in the long run, good television news is always substance over form. The relationship between talent—a term loosely applied to those who work on-air—and management is uneasy, at best. Talent argues that management has little appreciation for the complex, and often indefinable, factors that go into the communication of news. Management regards talent as overpriced prima donnas who want maximum ego gratification for minimum effort; no skills required. Just get out the cookie cutter and produce a batch of whatever is selling at the moment.

Television is intensely personal. Just *how* personal was emphasized when my associate, Leila Bright, told me about an elderly woman she had met at the Zion Baptist Church in Washington, D.C. Her favorite program was *The Beverly Hillbillies*. When the Hillbillies waved at the end of the show, she waved back. No matter what anyone told her to the contrary, she insisted that they were waving to *her*.

You can get someone to wear a Dan Rather sweater and do a Dan Rather delivery, but you won't have Dan Rather. Put a mustache on an avuncular, silver-haired man, and it still won't be trusty Uncle Walter. What is projected by the best newscasters is a third dimension—the essence of the personality and not the clothes or hair style.

A slew of newscasters went through a period of copying David Brinkley—the familiar angling of the body, the dipped head, the slightly sideways glance at the camera. When Tom Snyder caught on, he was cloned everywhere. I recall a local anchorman who emerged in California after Tom left Los Angeles for New York. If you turned your back and heard him speak, you would think, "Good heavens. Snyder's back." Newscasters such as Barbara Walters have been copied right down to their speech impediments.

When the ratings at Channel 3 in Philadelphia went up after I became co-anchor, the competitive station held open auditions to find a female who looked the most like me. They hired an elementary school teacher with no journalistic experience, had her hair cut like mine, bought her the same tailored jackets, and shoved her in front of the camera. She didn't last, of course, because rapport with the audience has nothing to do with blonde pageboys or blue blazers; to assume that it does merely trivializes the whole industry. That is what KYW general manager Alan Bell wrote to the woman who had written to him suggesting that he hire her daughter as an anchorwoman because she had *red* hair and would, therefore, make an appealingly different newscaster. That the daughter knew nothing about the business posed no problem for her mother. To an increasingly sophisticated audience, with visceral instincts for substance, it undoubtedly *would* have posed a problem.

The intimate relationship built up over time between an anchor and the viewers probably explains the results of a recent Harris survey of U.S. citizens: More than twice as many people trust national television news as trust their local newspapers. Television, according to Marshall McLuhan, is the modern-day tribal experience of our mobile society. The solid sense of place created by a succession of generations living and dying in the same town is fast becoming a relic of history, replaced by the community of the airwaves. Chet was there when Laura got her braces and when the Oakes boy next door got married. Walter and John and David stayed put when the family moved from Des Moines to Dubuque. The continuity of the newscasters' presence lends a stability to our lives—a constant in a society in which there are few constants. The news anchor is exactly that—an anchor, a center, a focus.

———————— • ————————

Anchoring is a way of guaranteeing a popular reporter consistent on-air exposure. Several reporters are assigned to cover stories throughout the day, but there is no way of determining which of those stories will actually be aired or which will have a prominent place in the newscast. News events cannot be controlled, nor can newscasts be mapped out like entertainment shows. Though reporters are assured of a fairly regular share of lead stories if they are given good beats—the

White House, for instance, generates leads with a certain predictability—anchors are always seen.

———————— • ————————

No working day can be described as entirely typical for an anchor. Sometimes my most pressing task is simply to tend to my mail. Viewers write to complain about the color of the blouse I wore two nights before or to compliment me on a story. They offer and ask for advice, propose marriage, wonder if I will mate my Siberian Husky, Chewy. They send hand-knit ski caps and homemade Christmas ornaments and cotton panties with the seven days of the week stitched across the bottom. Some address me as "female anchorman." I read and answer every letter personally—with the help of my assistant, Jered Dawaliby—unless they are obviously psychotic ramblings.

During the week I am usually up by 7:00 to run in the park with Chewy. The rest of the morning is spend reading the *New York Times,* the *Wall Street Journal,* the *Washington Post,* and either the *New York Post* or the *Daily News,* which are delivered in a bundle to my door. I also read a paper from some other American city, preferably not in the top ten, selected at random. By the time I get to my office, I know all the major news stories of the day. At NBC, I then read the wire stories from AP, UPI, and Reuters, as well as the satellite feeds coming in from our correspondents abroad. If possible, I listen to at least one all-news radiocast.

In midafternoon I meet with Executive Producer Tom Wolzien, Associate Producer Bill Chesleigh, Field Producers Joe Alicastro, Ken Bell, Richard Berman, Susan Dutcher, Cheryl Gould, Eve Krzyzanowski, Director Marvin Einhorn, Associate Directors Judy Farinet and Katherine Powers, Unit Manager Marilyn Gelefsky, News and Feature Assistant Amy Sue Levin, Researcher Ann Terrien, Production Assistant Joan Bradley, and Production Secretary Cindy Fraust. We discuss the final rundown: what stories will be included in the newscast or on *Update*, where they will be placed, and how long they will be. The rundown is never final. Anything can be changed right up to air time, depending on breaking stories.

At approximately 4:00, I begin writing my script. If I am working on a special report or there are late-breaking developments, Richard Berman or Richard Watt writes and I edit.

Most anchors write their own copy and select what is known as close pad material for the end of the newscast. I worked with an anchorman in Philadelphia who, during his short tenure at KYW, always came up with cuter, funnier, more interesting close pads than I did. What puzzled me was how I could continue to miss these items in all the newspapers and magazines I scoured throughout the day. Finally, I begged him to tell me where the hell he was getting his information.

"I make it up," he said.

"You mean none of these things ever *happened?*"

"No . . . but they *should* have."

On Saturday evenings, I go downstairs to the makeup department at about 5:30, and at 8:00 on weekdays. Both my half-hour newscast and *Update* air in the old site of the Howdy Doody peanut gallery where I longed to sit as a little girl.

When my day ends around 10:00, I usually head straight home by cab, eat a light dinner, and watch the 11:00 news. Television sets dominate my study, living room, and bedroom, all of them, more often than not, tuned to three different channels at once. Outside of work, I spend whatever spare time is left with a small circle of close friends, or with my family.

Although I live alone except for Chewy and my two cats, Sveltie and Rommie, I have a reliable support system. Long ago, when I had wrung all the toothpaste I could out of the tube I had meant to replace for a week, I knew I needed household help. I have a part-time housekeeper who shops, cooks and cleans. Susan Erenburg of NBC's wardrobe department helps organize my on-air clothes. A neighboring tenant's twelve-year-old son, Gregg Smith, walks the dog and feeds the cats when I am away or tied up at NBC. My assistant, Jered, my researcher, David Buda, and my business manager, Robert Andrews, organize the day-to-day details of my job and finances. Robyn Capazzi of

Andrews Management books my outside speeches and appearances. I intentionally live near the bureau to save commuting time. The bonus is that when I have to skip my calisthenics class, I can exercise by briskly walking to and from work.

———— • ————

The single life is not one I willingly choose for myself. I have a need for a foundation, although, like most female anchors I know, I remained single long past the point when my peers had begun to build families. Jane Pauley married Gary Trudeau when she was thirty; Judy Woodruff, now in her mid-thirties, married to *Wall Street Journal* reporter Al Hunt, had their first child only this year.

An anchorwoman has two choices of men: those who date her because of her job, and those who date her in spite of it. A man has to be strong enough to deal with the recognizability—my late husband joked that he didn't mind being called Dr. Savitch as long as he wasn't called Mr. Jessica—and the unintentional rejections. In our culture, saying "I have to work late" is another way of saying "I'm not interested in you."

I went into the industry knowing it would be more time-consuming and stress-provoking than the average career. I knew I was biting off a big chunk, but I didn't know just *how* big. The catchwords of my profession are commitment and sac-

rifice. I couldn't have married in my twenties
because both my marriage and my career would
have suffered. My personal life could not have
borne the weight of my professional ambition, and
I needed mobility; to move up in the profession is
to move out. Two-career families in this business
have the same struggles as those in any industry.
When a husband gets his big break and can leave
Tucson for Denver, traditionally his wife packs up
the kids and furniture and heads out too. But
what if the anchor tapped for a move up the lad-
der happens to be female? Will her husband leave
his comfortable career niche and seek his fortune
on her new turf?

In interviews I gave early on in my career, I was
quoted as saying it was possible to have it all: a
dynamic job, marriage, and children. But after
years of struggling make it to the top I had begun to wonder if it was possible to combine a fully
satisfying personal life with a successful career.
Clearly it is now possible for a woman to get and
hold a significant job in broadcast journalism, to
succeed or fail based on the sum and substance of
her talent and dedication. Whether she can inte-
grate that success into a workable social framework is in large part up to her relationships with
others and the serendipitous winds of chance. It
may well not be probable for one to simultaneously experience fulfillment personally and professionally, but the *possibility* leads me on.

In some respects, I was what you might call a

social adolescent. Since everything for me had always been a major commitment, I didn't have casual affairs or even casual friendships. My first serious romantic attachment had been with Ron Kershaw, and I was almost twenty-three years old when I met him. As I entered my thirties, I was seized with an overpowering urgency to strike a balance.

On a January morning in 1980, I was married, at the age of thirty-one, to a Philadelphia advertising executive. After a traditional ceremony at the Plaza Hotel in New York, I went off on a cross-country trip—alone. Campaign '80 and my marriage began simultaneously. Some weeks the only glimpse my husband caught of me was on television. John Chancellor once joked that, in an election year, he kisses his wife goodbye just after Christmas and kisses her hello again after the inauguration. That may have worked for the Chancellors, but it didn't for us.

I followed candidates all day long, and while they rested I kept working into the evening, writing and editing my stories to feed to the evening news or preparing for the next day's nonstop events. There was scarcely time to even phone home. My husband and I saw each other on an average of twice a month, and before the year ended we made a mutual decision to not so much end our marriage as to not begin it. The separation was not strictly a casualty of my schedule. I had been naive enough to think I could build a lasting relationship out of mutual respect and friendship, to think I could create a storybook life without working at it. It had not occurred to me that marriage requires the same effort as a career. And unlike a career, a marriage requires a joint effort.

———————— • ————————

Soon after our divorce, I met the man who was to become my second husband, Dr. Donald Rollie Payne—a physician from Washington, D.C. We were introduced by a mutual friend who was visiting me one evening when I was being treated for a minor medical ailment. We fell deeply in love, and were quietly married in the spring of 1981. For the first time in my life, I thought I was going to have it all. We both worked at our careers. We both enjoyed the mutual efforts we put into making our marriage work.

We planned to start a family immediately and bought a townhouse big enough to accommodate his four sons from a previous marriage on their weekend visits. I was four months pregnant when the first of my bubbles burst. The child was not to be born. Shortly thereafter, my husband died.

When I returned to work, the viewers were a great source of support. One message read: "We are so glad that you're OK. Don't ever get lost again." The underlying tone was: "Don't let it snow in Camelot. Be in reality what you seem to be on the newscast." For those thirty minutes, newscasters are indeed in control; but there are twenty-three and a half more hours in every day, over which we have varying degrees of control—depending on the ebb and flow of life. Success brings success. It does not necessarily bring happiness.

At the end of September, 1981, I asked Bill Small, then NBC News President (he was replaced by Reuven Frank), to transfer me to New York. The Washington Bureau was down the street from the house in which Don died, and I wanted to escape all the memories. I was still getting my new office sorted out when I got a call from Bob Rogers, one of the best-known and most highly respected documentary producers in television. "Reading, Writing and Reefer," his definitive work on the uses and abuses of marijuana, has become a classic. For two years Bob had been working on a documentary about KGB surveillance in the United States. I was still visibly shaken by my grief, so choosing me to work with him on "Spies Among Us" was a calculated risk. My assignment and Bob's support helped me get through some of the worst moments of a very bad period. I had almost forgotten how much fun it was to be involved in a story; the documentary revived my faith in the business and in my career.

Only once did I think I might not make it through. Several weeks after I left Washington I found myself back on Embassy Row, to do an interview. I maintained my composure as we drove past my old neighborhood, but as soon as I got to the embassy I ran for the ladies' room and burst into tears. I will be unendingly grateful to producer Patricia Creaghan, who calmly told me to take all the time I needed and then told the interview subject and the crew that the correspondent was reviewing her research material and would be along shortly.

"Spies Among Us" was well-received, winning acclaim from the Foreign Relations Committee, the White House, reviewers and, most importantly, from what we affectionately call the Average Viewer. It would have been a wonderful assignment for any correspondent; for me, it was a godsend.

I do not mean to suggest that my personal difficulties should be taken as a measure of what women going into the industry can expect. My own particular set of circumstances is no more a standard than the overdrawn or distorted female news characters of the silver screen, who are never shown running their stockings or ripping their nails on the wire machines. *The China Syndrome*, *Airport*, and *Network* perpetuated several industry myths: Women reporters get too emotionally involved with the men they are assigned to cover; women are too emotional to cover news in the first place; women are more concerned with their looks than with their news judgment; women can make it to the top, but only if they are cold, brittle, and ruthless. For me, the truth has always been somewhere between the dream and a harsher reality. And like most women in the business, I feel an obligation to live down the most unrealistic aspects of the myths while forging a path of my own. But as fast as newswomen live down those myths, new ones keep cropping up. The latest wrinkle is on wrinkles. It seems there is a widespread belief that women can't grow old in television news; that there will be no female counterpart to Uncle Walter, no strong mother image to balance the older, authoritative father figure in television news reporting. Barely a decade into being afforded a beginning in this field, women reporters are being asked what will happen when they grow old.

As to why the previous crop of female correspondents—Dickerson, Frederick, McLaughlin, et al—seemed to lose career momentum as they grew older, the answer is in the quality and quantity of their air time, or rather the lack of it. The first wave of women newscasters did not anchor. They were not seen with predictable frequency in key assignments. There was little chance for them to inspire and foster viewer allegiance. It is likely that some of today's female correspondents, given the same amount of access to viewers as their male colleagues, will engender the type of viewer loyalty that permits one to grow old on television. It will have to do with proven skills, not irrelevant sexual characteristics.

Chapter
17

Not long ago a close friend in Washington, Jean Sylvester, saw her two daughters, Kate, seven, and Meg, three, playing television newscasters in the back yard. The microphone they were using was a turkey baster turned upside down. I never thought about doing anything with a turkey baster except baste a turkey. The rules of the game changed in my generation, and my career paralleled that transition.

There has been significant progress. Just this year, *Weekend Nightly News* producer Bill Chesleigh found himself at the 4 P.M. rundown meeting with not only a female anchor but also a female director—Judith Farinet—plus women editors, domestic news producers, production assistants and associates, and a woman heading the foreign desk.

All of the women present had agreed beforehand that as soon as Chesleigh said, "OK, Segment One," we would whip out pocket mirrors, nail files, lipsticks, powder puffs—all manner of feminine accouterments. In spite of himself, Ches had to laugh. A sure signal that we have indeed come a long way if we can take our jobs, but not ourselves, so seriously.

When I was a little girl growing up in Kennett Square, Pennsylvania, it would never have occurred to me to say I want to be a television correspondent. I never, until high school, saw a woman correspondent. When I first anchored in 1970, I had never seen a woman anchor a news show. All of the little girls in my class, when asked what it was they wanted to be when they grew up, said one of three things—a nurse, a teacher, or a mommy. Not that there was anything wrong with any of those professions. But they were the only ones we chose, because they were the only ones for which we had role models. The sole alternatives were TV and movie role models. We could have elected to have become cowgirls like Dale Evans.

When I first became a reporter, the spokesperson on any given story was almost invariably a white male. Over the years, the political representative, attorney, medical spokesperson, scientist, or governmental official was more and more likely to be female—perhaps black or some other minority. The stated message was that which the story contained. The implied message, the one received by young girls growing up, is, "Here is a woman in that job. I will be a woman someday. I could have that job." Black and other minority children draw the same conclusions from minorities observed in the power structure. Young white males observing a woman or a black on television tend to grow up accepting minorities as equals.

Back in the early seventies, when I was starting out as an anchor in Houston, I was interviewed by a local newspaper reporter who asked me how it felt to be a leader in the women's movement. I was stunned. It had never been my intention to lead *any* movement. I had merely set out to be a television journalist, and in the process I became an inadvertent pioneer and was given the unrequested mantle of role model. Covering the news in these complex, turbulent times is a grave responsibility. Add to that the title Role Model, and the responsibility becomes almost crushingly awesome. It implies you not only do your job proficiently, you handle every other aspect of your life with exemplary skill. The seekers of role models, I am afraid, often envision a whole perfect life to go along with the relatively flawless thirty-minute newscast. Being a novelty, one of the first females to successfully hold down a job in what was traditionally an all-male field, does not imbue one with super powers in other aspects of life.

Being a novelty had its advantages. Even though the women emerging in television news today don't have the same obstacles to overcome as the women of my era, they face a different set of problems. There is more competition for fewer jobs. Historically, when the economy gets tight, such sociological issues as minority hiring are pushed to the background. The rush to place women in the power structure is winding down; everybody is more interested in turning a profit.

Although we've come a long way after a late start, there are not that many of us at the top of the line. We're not yet equal in number to men, but the huge discrepancy has diminished. A decade ago, only a handful of women were prominent in the news: Marya McLaughlin at CBS; Marlene Saunders, who broke the network anchor barrier briefly in the mid-sixties at ABC; Liz Trotta, the first woman to cover a war, at NBC. About the same time I was hired as a gofer at CBS, a brilliant newspaper journalist, Mary Pangalos, was hired as a street reporter. Mary had won a Pulitzer Prize for a *Newsday* series on organized crime, and she could have been one of CBS's shining stars had she been given a chance. It was a little like throwing fresh meat before wolves. Mary had not been trained in television techniques, and she would go on location with cameramen who would later tell her, back at the studio, that the film hadn't turned out. What happened to women behind the scenes who were trying to break into the industry was much the same. There was no upfront discrimination; they simply were not trained. Since the midseventies, however, I have occasionally worked with an all-female crew—field producer, camerawoman, and sound technician.

Men still control the news, both on and off camera. Decisions are made in the executive suites, the last area to be penetrated by women. With exceptions like Amy McCombs, general manager of WDIV, the Post-Newsweek station in Detroit, and Judith Girard, program director of WTAE-TV in Pittsburgh, women who ascend to upper-level management often have titles but no discernible power.

On-air women are by and large relegated to weekends, co-anchoring with males at 5:30 or 6:30, or softer interview shows. Most of us who do straight news prefer it to news-talk shows, although I rather enjoy filling in on the *Today Show*.

Women who have anchored election night coverage—Lesley Stahl, Cassie Mackin, Barbara Walters—have more than held their own, but, as NBC Vice President Don Meaney pointed out in *Ms.* magazine, "A woman reporter almost by definition is likely to be junior to men who are doing that kind of thing. She might feel deferential, and men might not be too kind." Meaney, however, went on to add that "The deference and the animosity is changing."

The first night Lesley Stahl covered the elections, she sat at a desk with name plates that read, Cronkite, Rather, Mudd, Female. This past spring, Lesley was quoted on an anecdote about her Watergate coverage when she did cross talks with Daniel Schorr and Dan Rather after the evening newscast. The three of them stood in front of the great wood-paneled Senate hearing room and discussed what had transpired that day in the ongoing drama. That is, Dan and Dan did. Lesley couldn't get a word in edgewise. After a couple of nights, it was suggested by the powers that be that it would be nice if Lesley had an opportunity to comment. That evening Walter Cronkite asked about all the gossip flying around Capitol Hill. Dan and Dan politely waited for Lesley to take over, but Lesley had decided a gossip question was one best avoided by a woman. Finally Daniel Schorr spoke up and said, "Since that's a gossip story and we have a woman here, why don't we let Lesley handle that one?" She recalled that she blathered a bit, and when the interview ended, she said good night to everyone, and made a beeline to the phone to call her parents.

"Daddy! I was terrible, wasn't I?"

"Honey, you were terrific! You really pulled it off. We're so proud of you."

"You're not telling me the truth. Put mother on."

"Oh. Look, honey, she can't come to the phone right now."

"Why not?"

"Well . . . she's in the bathroom crying."

In retrospect, the story was funny. But only because things are genuinely changing for the better. Women may not have it easy, but we are given a fairer chance to reach for the top.

———————— • ————————

Once a year I teach an intensive, one-week broadcasting course at Ithaca College, which has given me a seat on the board of trustees and an honorary doctorate. The question I am most often asked in my classroom is, "How can I get a job in television?" I repeat Dan Rather's advice: "I always encourage them not to try. The ones who go ahead anyway will probably succeed."

But I have to gently introduce them to the cold, hard statistical reality: Perhaps two, at the most, out of their class, will get a job. The television industry does not have unlimited allocated frequencies, like franchises for a fast food chain. The job market for anchors and reporters is closing up. Despite the advent of cable, the post–Watergate interest in the reporting field combined with the lifting of requirements on minority hiring has made competition stiff.

I can offer no formula for breaking into television. A good broad-based education is a major tool, and then it is necessary to go out and learn the trade by doing. Learn to write. Learn to interview. Learn to care about what you write and how you interview, and not just how the news is presented. Learn that television news is a delicate balance of serving public good and private gain. Dedicate yourself to understanding the difference. Draw the line between the two and stick to the public good.

We're training people who look and sound good on television. But there is more to newscasting than mastering the mechanics. News reading and news reporting are separate skills. News reading is not to be ridiculed—not everybody can do it—but events unfold that have to be reported spontaneously, without a script. John Chancellor says it's like being a preacher: Ninety percent of the time it's services as usual. Then the moment comes when late-breaking news dictates understanding and depth over mere reading ability. Conversely, it doesn't matter a whit how fine a reporter you are if you can't communicate.

My worst fear is that too many young people are attracted to television news for the wrong reasons. I asked one of my students why she wanted to go into broadcasting and she answered, "So I can make a million dollars." She didn't want to be a reporter; she wanted to be rich. A drama student said if she didn't make it as an actress, she would become an anchor. "But they're not the same thing," I said. "No, but they're both *stars*," she chirped.

The glossy image of newscasting is largely illusory. More realistically, it is commitment and dedication and hard work. The 6:30 news must go on at 6:30. You can't be five minutes late, or say, "I'm not up to it tonight. I'll do two newscasts tomorrow."

It also means, because you report a story, you are supposed to have an answer on how to solve it. Thus, one sees network correspondents delivering speeches to the local chamber of commerce being asked, "Do you think the president should make further cuts in the social security program?" Or, "What policy should the United States be following in El Salvador?" Or my favorite question ever asked by an audience, "Do you think Western Civilization, overall, has been a success?"

Television newscasters do not cause an event. Theirs is to give you a fair report on how it's going. Still, as the Egyptian pharaohs gave the messenger who brought good news a reward and handed the bearer of bad tidings his head, so viewers tend to hold reporters responsible for bad news and expect them to change the events that caused them. Television newscasters are not the larger-than-life, disembodied heads they sometimes appear to be. They are subject to the same frailties and foibles that beset each of us. They hold no magic blueprint for the nation's future, or even sometimes, for their own.

In every interview I have ever read or seen or taken part in, the final question in our future-oriented society is always "What next?"

Interviewee: So then I patented the cure for

	cancer, negotiated a settlement in the Falklands, and singlehandedly wiped out inner-city crime.
Interviewer:	What next? Got any new projects going?
Interviewee:	Uh, I thought I'd take a little time off . . . maybe rest for a while.
Interviewer:	Yeah, but what are you going to *do*?

The message is clear: No matter how many goals you have achieved, you must set your sights on a higher one. My friend Mort Crim once told me there are two dangers in life: One is not getting what you want; the other is getting it. My current goal is to place a moratorium on goals, to enjoy an expanding, dynamic field with its widening potential for women.

Despite the hardships and sacrifices, it is an industry of many rewards, satisfying in a way just high-gloss promotion and high-dollar incomes never can be. All it takes is focusing—not down the hall at management or across the street at the competition—but through the screen. News reporting is a cycle: No matter how much you work at sending a message, it's only successful if it's received. As Thoreau said, "It takes two to speak the truth—one to speak, and another to hear."

Just when I'm on the verge of throwing up my hands and saying, "Is this all there is?" I hear from someone who says, "You reached me. You touched me. You made a difference in my life."

A viewer named Frances Adams sent a Polaroid snapshot of her mother-in-law, Ruth Adams, in Chester Depot, Vermont, watching me on television. "I thought you might enjoy the enclosed picture of yourself at my mother-in-law's house," she wrote. "Mrs. Adams is in her seventies, with poor hearing and failing vision. However, she is still able to enjoy television. She is a delightful lady, with a keen and youthful mind, so it is especially important to her that news broadcasts such as yours are available. They serve as a link to a world she can no longer see or hear very well. My husband took this picture on Thanksgiving morning. We think it tells a story, and we wanted to share it with you."

It is that sharing that makes the cycle complete.